CW01332871

Published in the UK by
POWERFRESH Limited
3 Gray Street
Northampton
NN1 3QQ

Telephone 01604 30996
Facsimile   01604 21013

Copyright © 1996 Colin Eyre and David Hallamshire

Cover and interior layout by Powerfresh

Peeping Tom

ISBN 1 874125 58 9

All rights reserved. No part of this publication may be
reproduced or transmitted in any form or by any means, electronic or mechanical,
 including photocopying, recording or any information storage and retrieval system,
or for the source of ideas without the written permission of the publisher.

Printed in the UK by Avalon Print Northampton
     Powerfresh September 1996

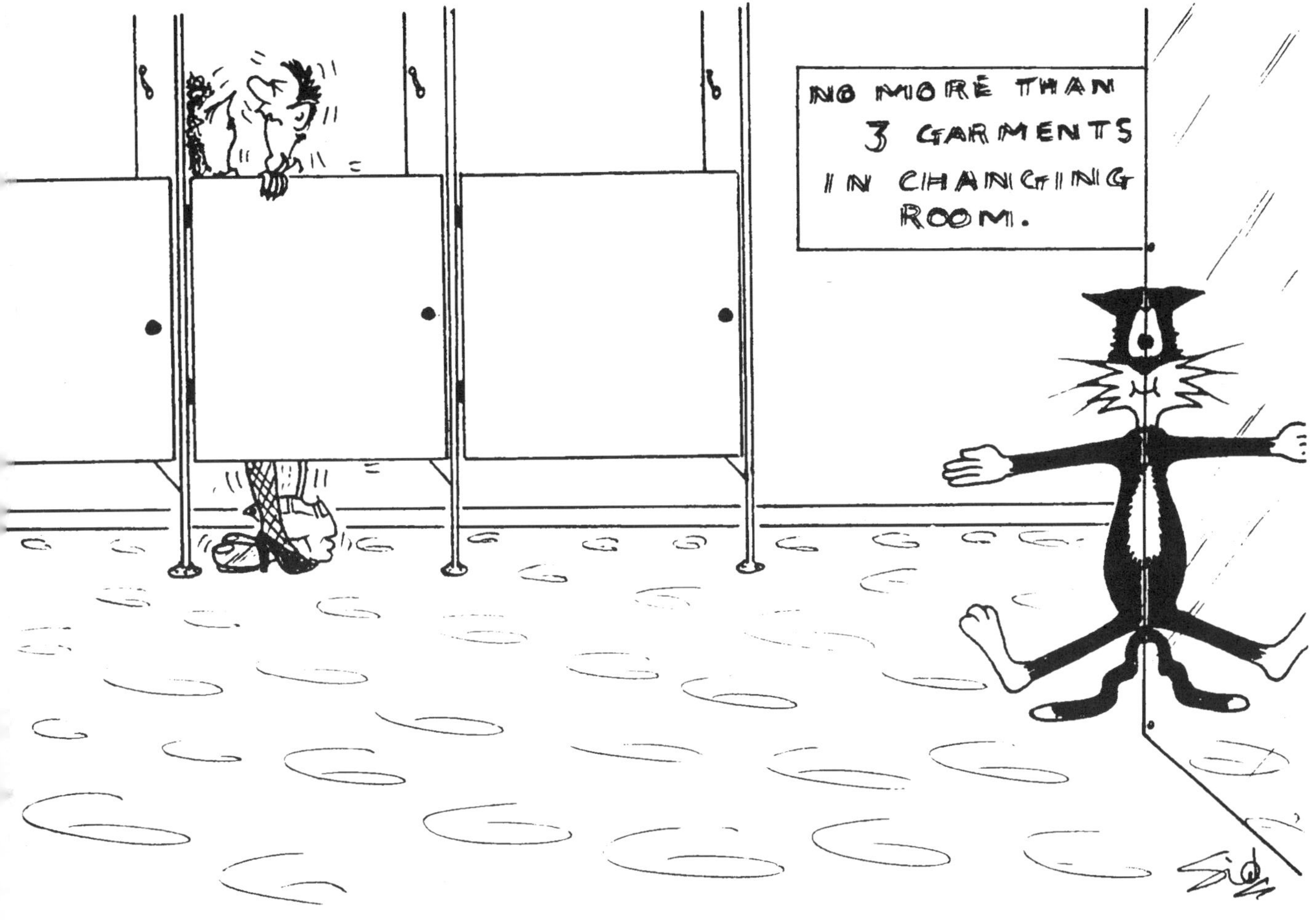
NO MORE THAN 3 GARMENTS IN CHANGING ROOM.

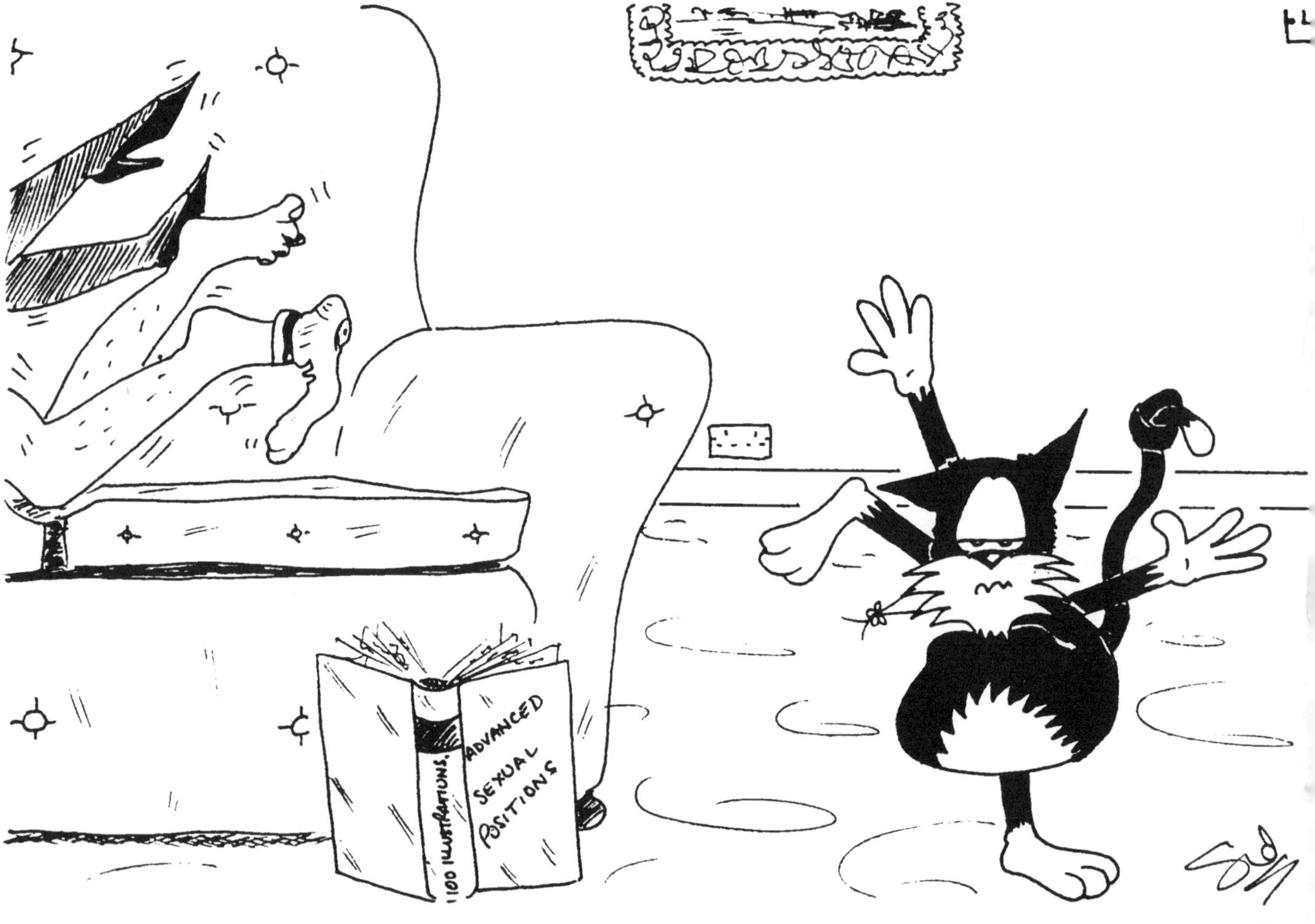
ADVANCED SEXUAL POSITIONS
100 ILLUSTRATIONS.

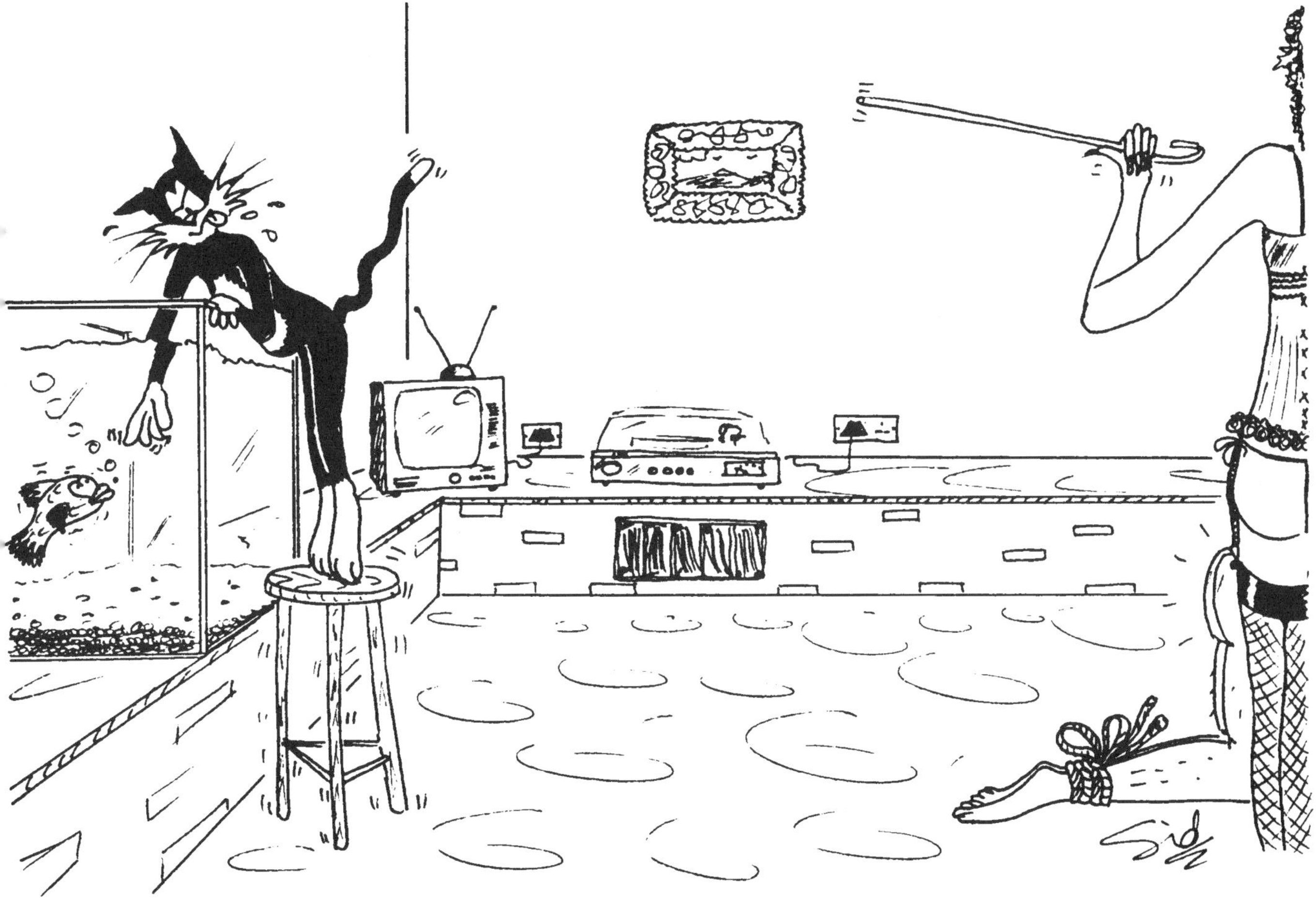
Sid

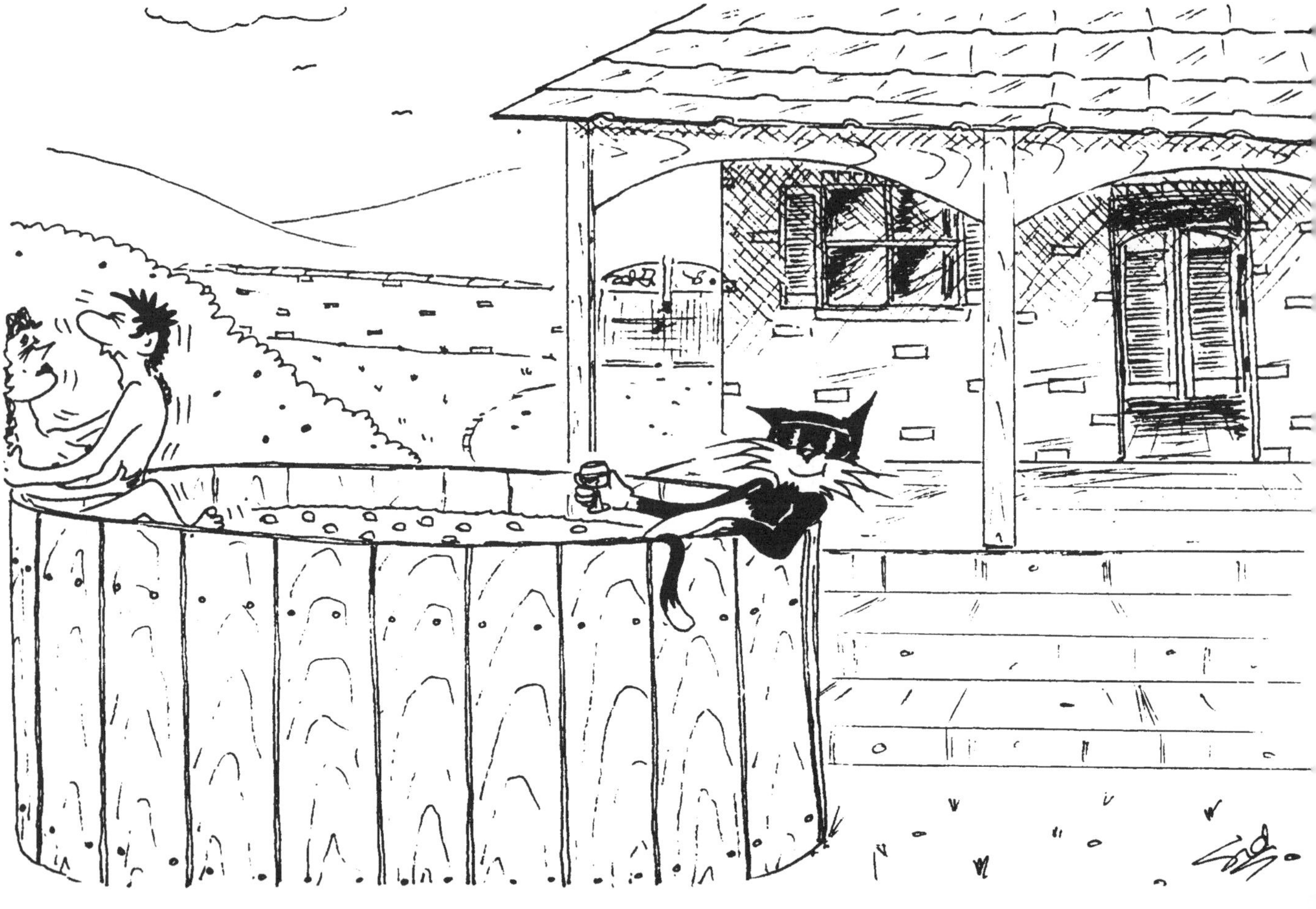

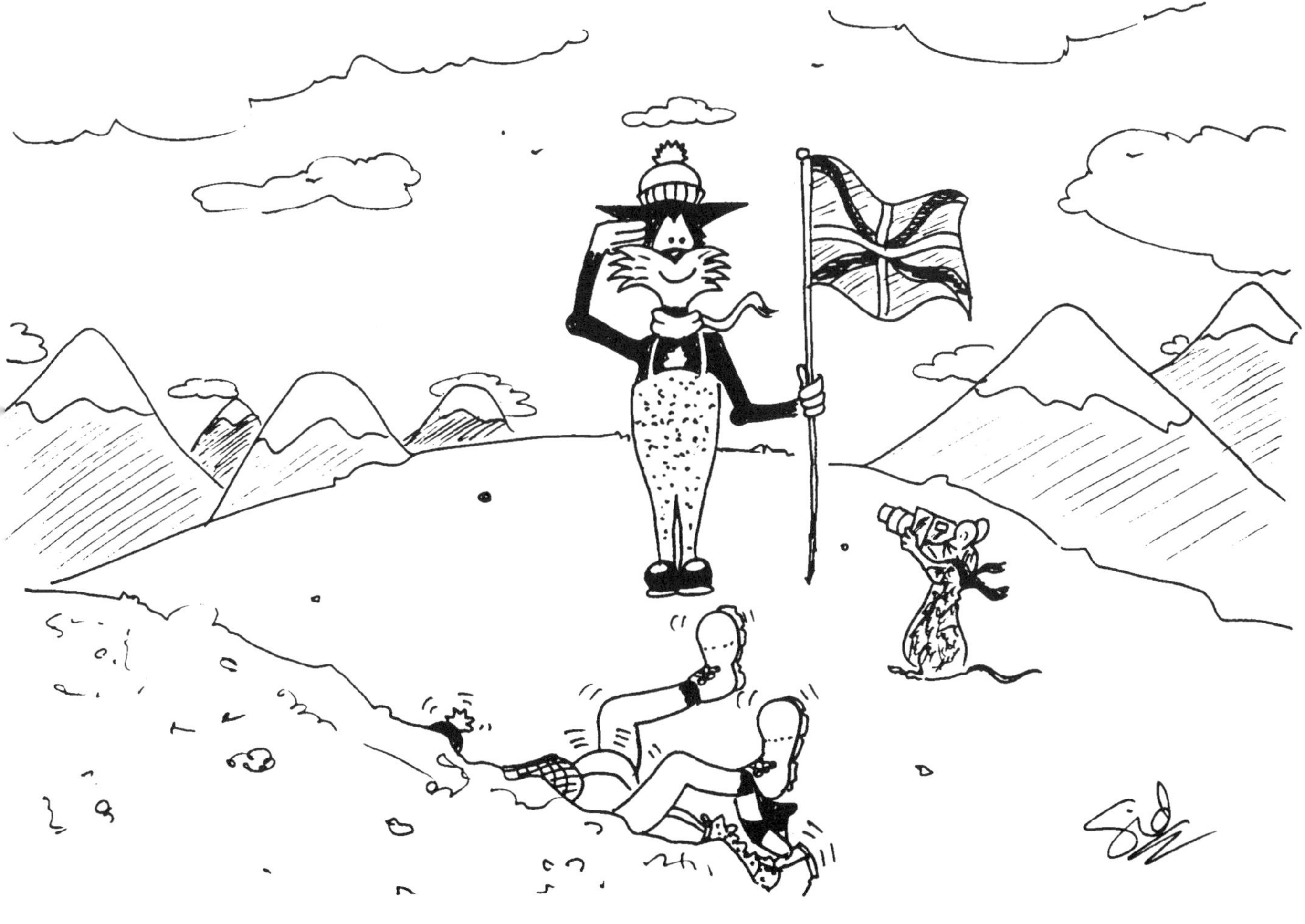
Sid

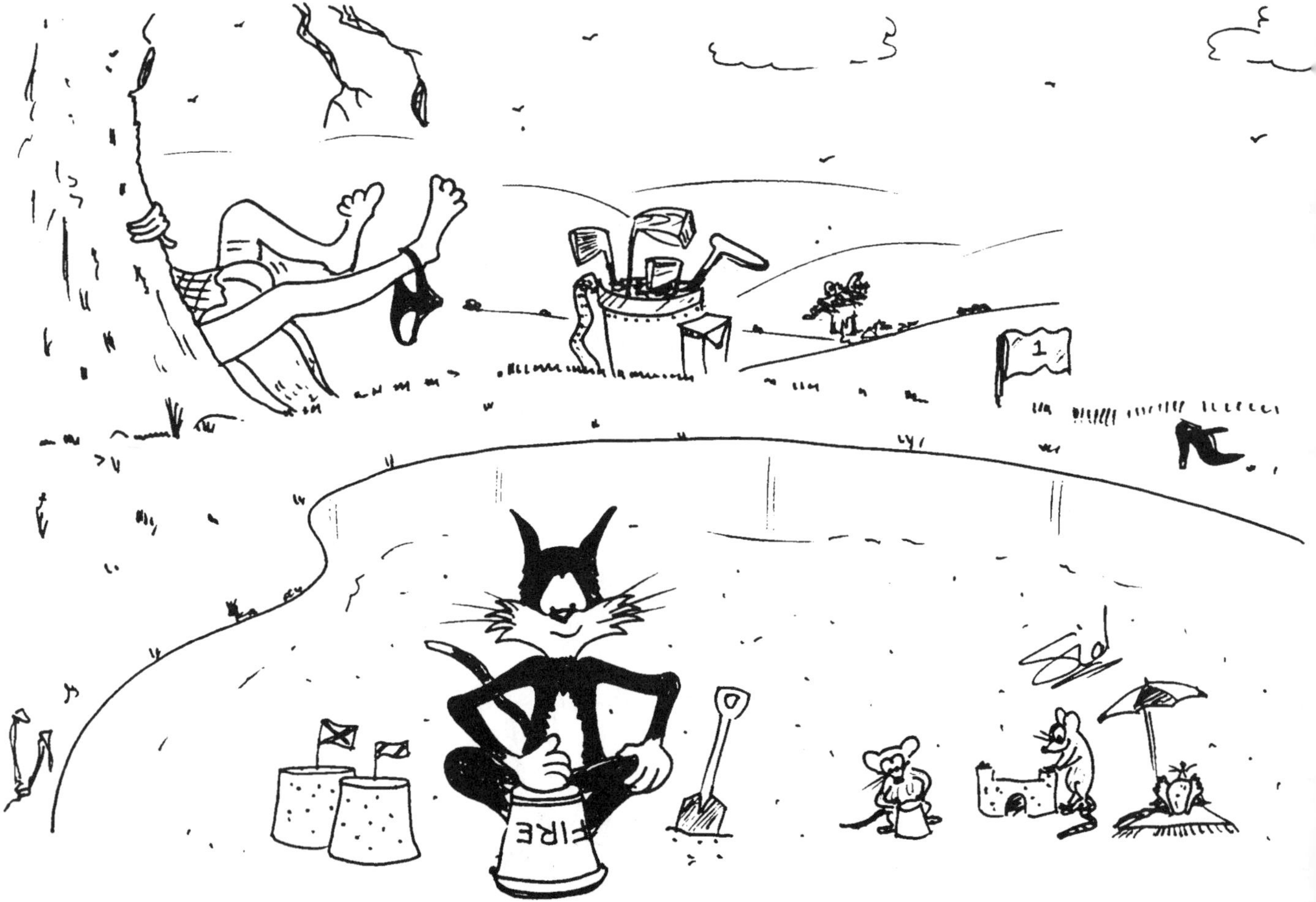
1
FIRE

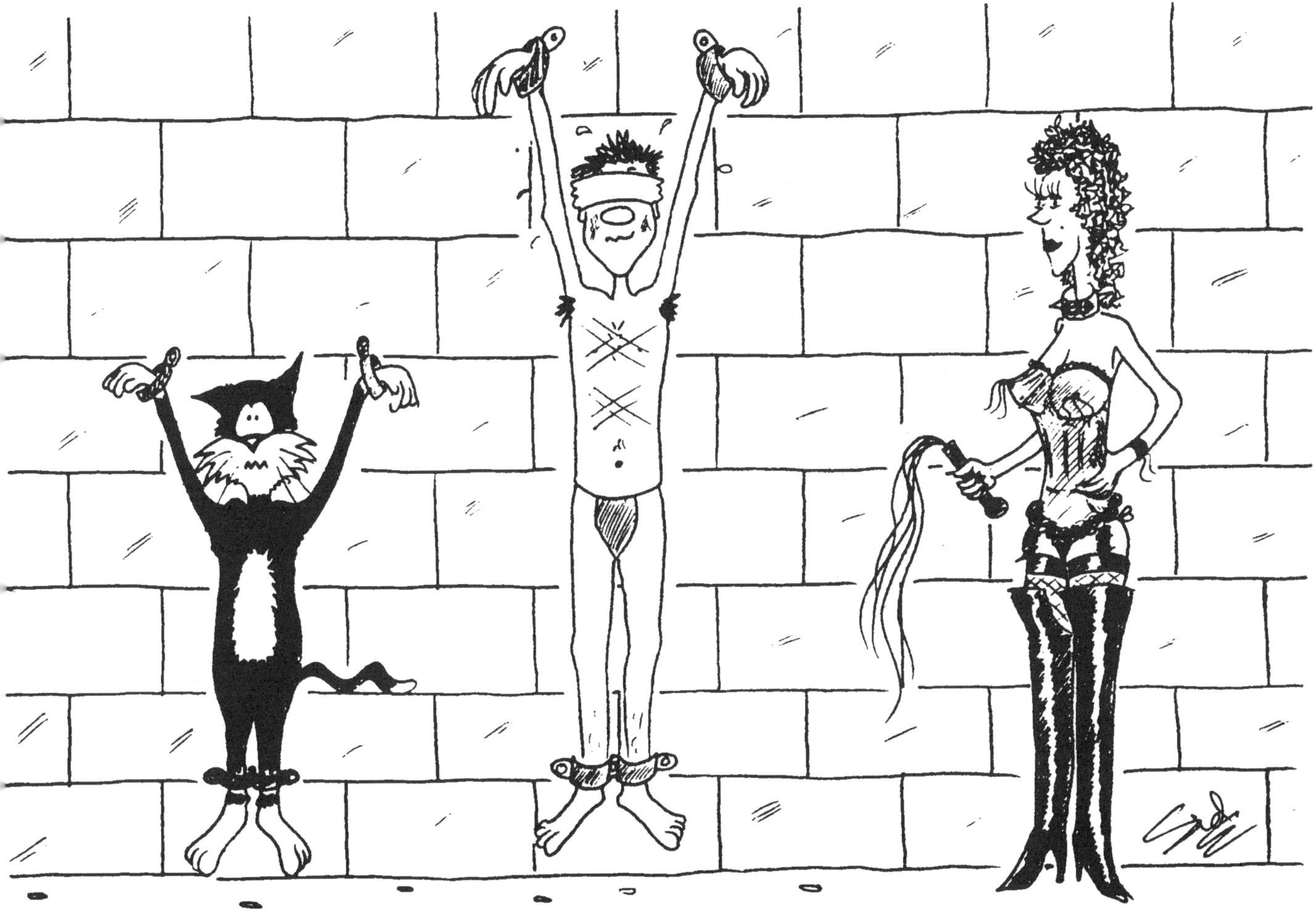

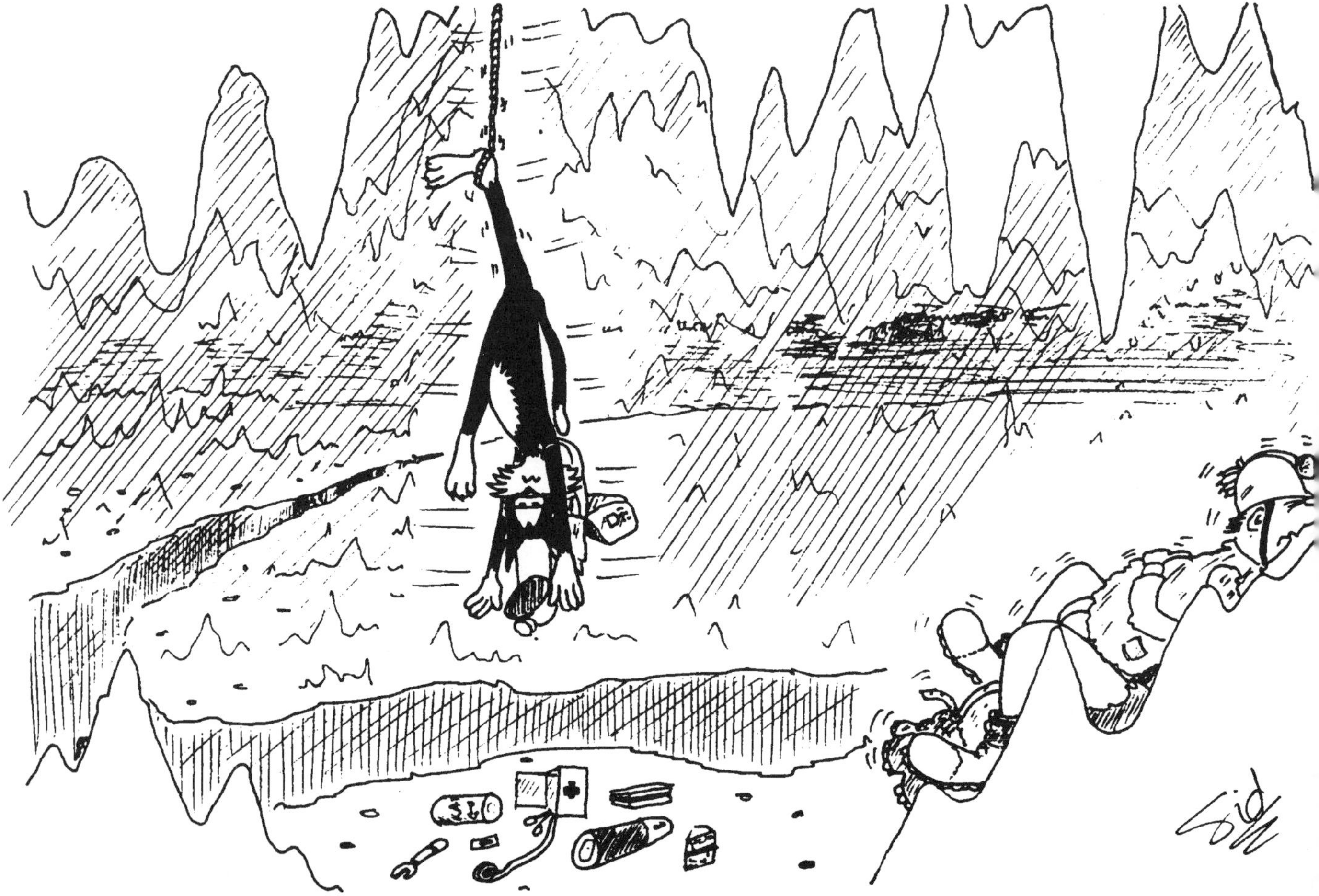

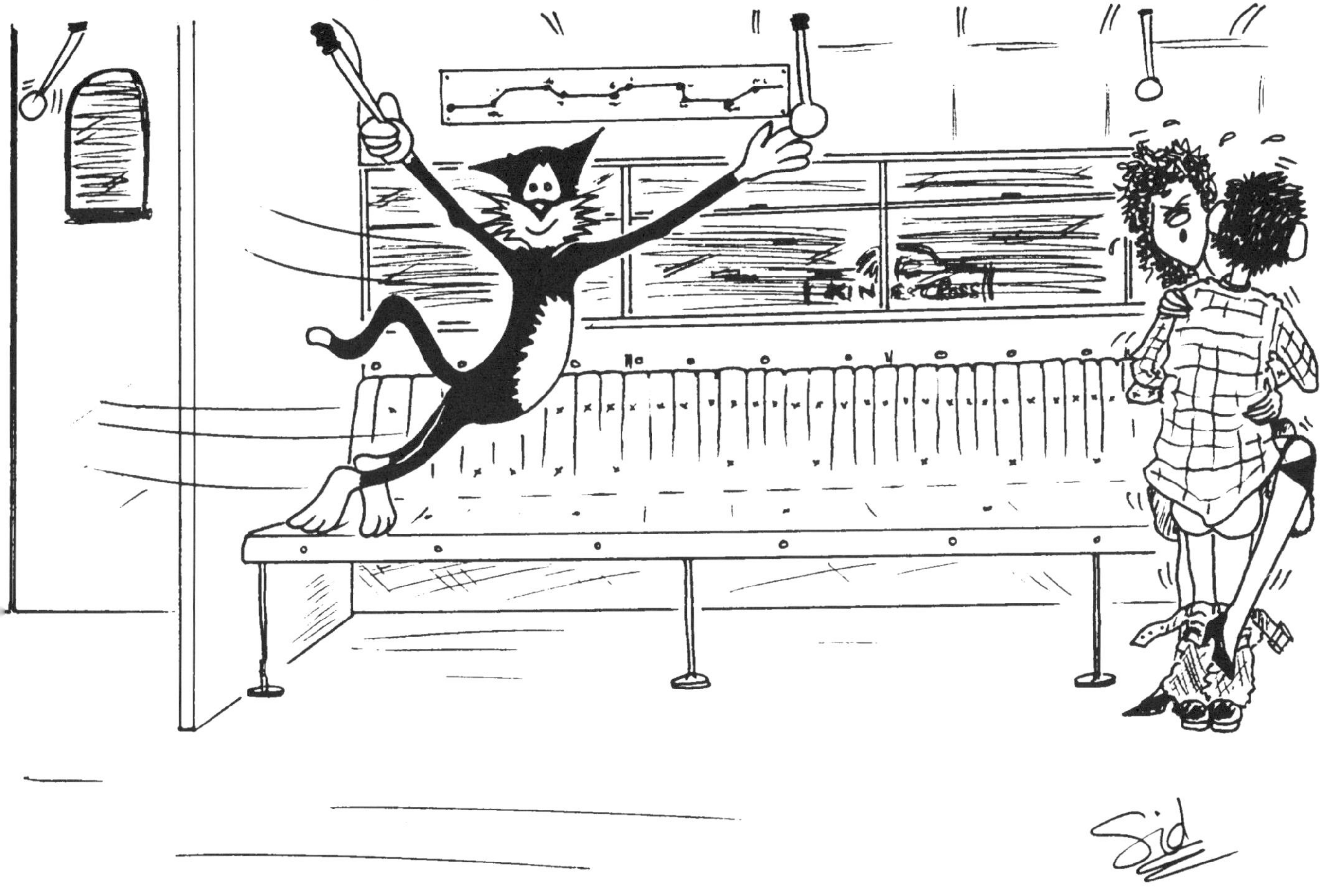
Sid

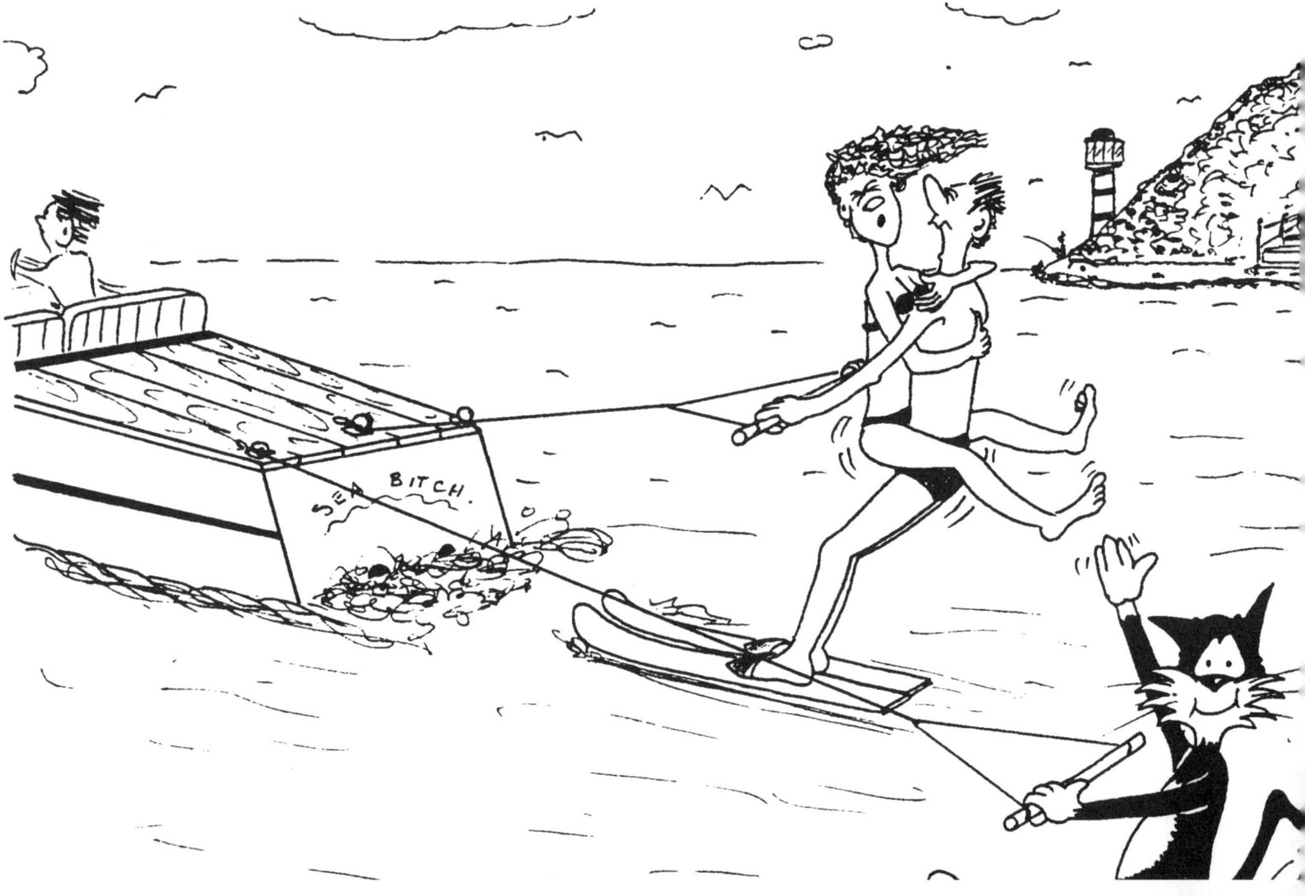
SEA BITCH.

POOL ROOM.

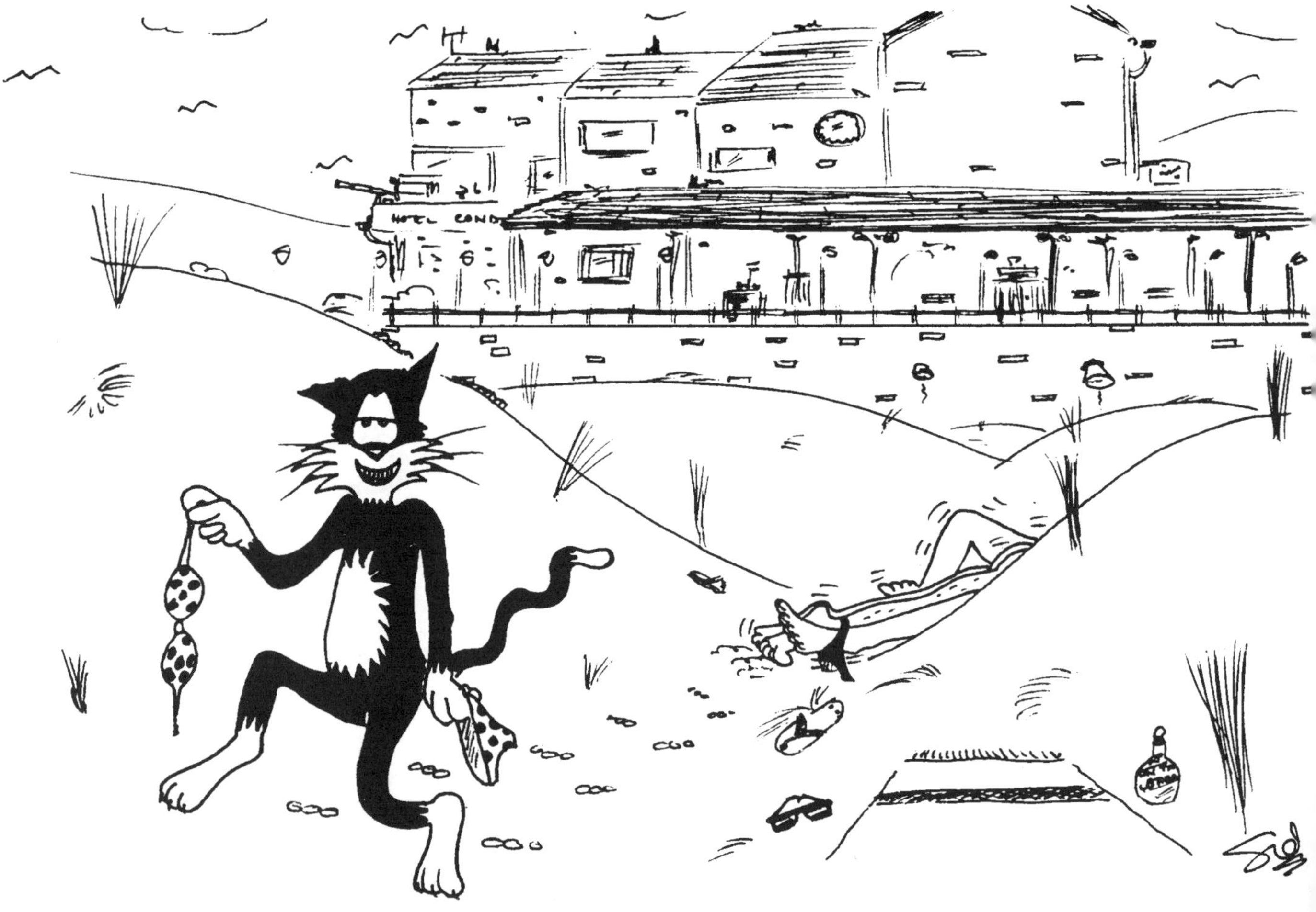
HOTEL COND

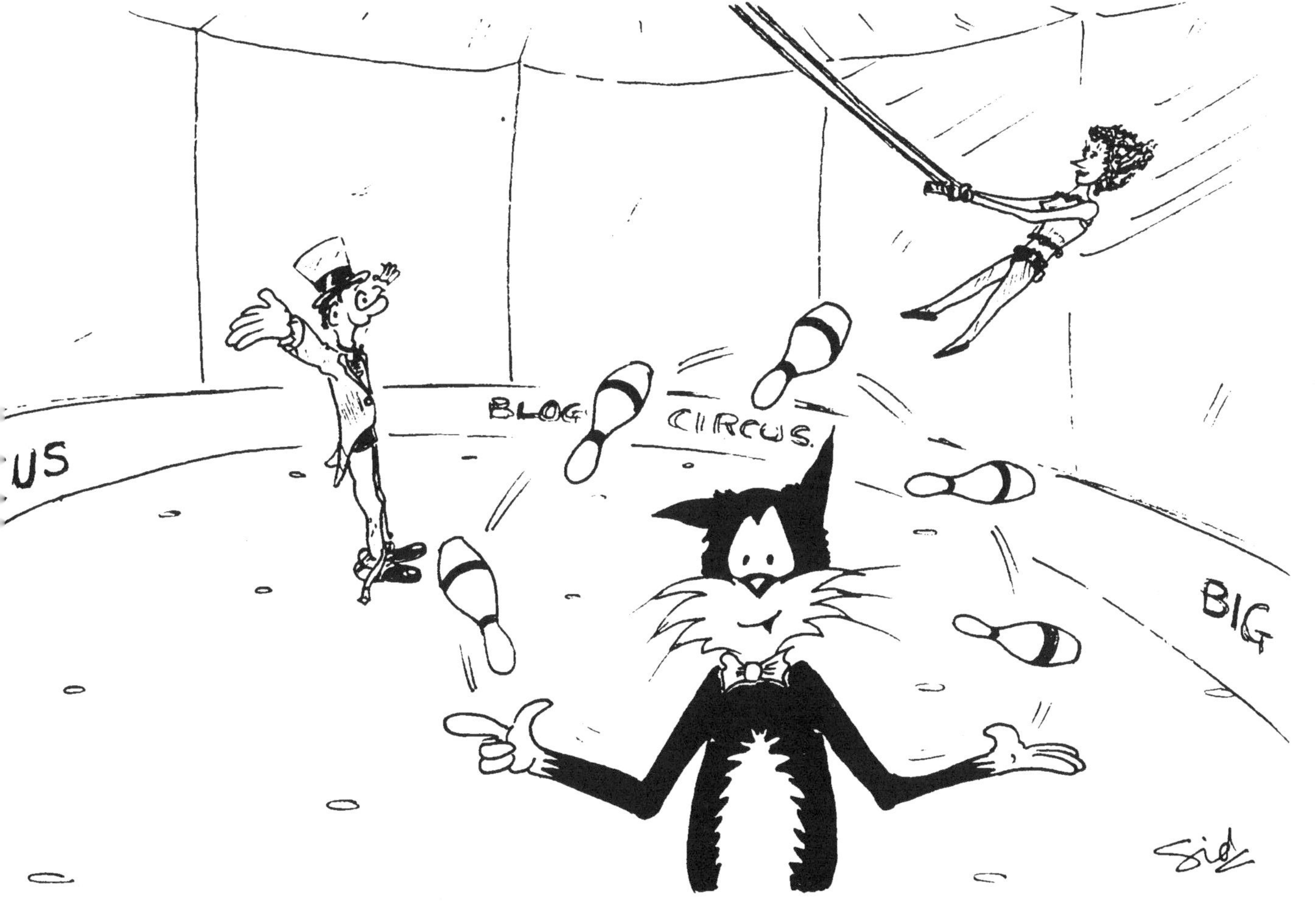

US
BLOG
CIRCUS.
BIG

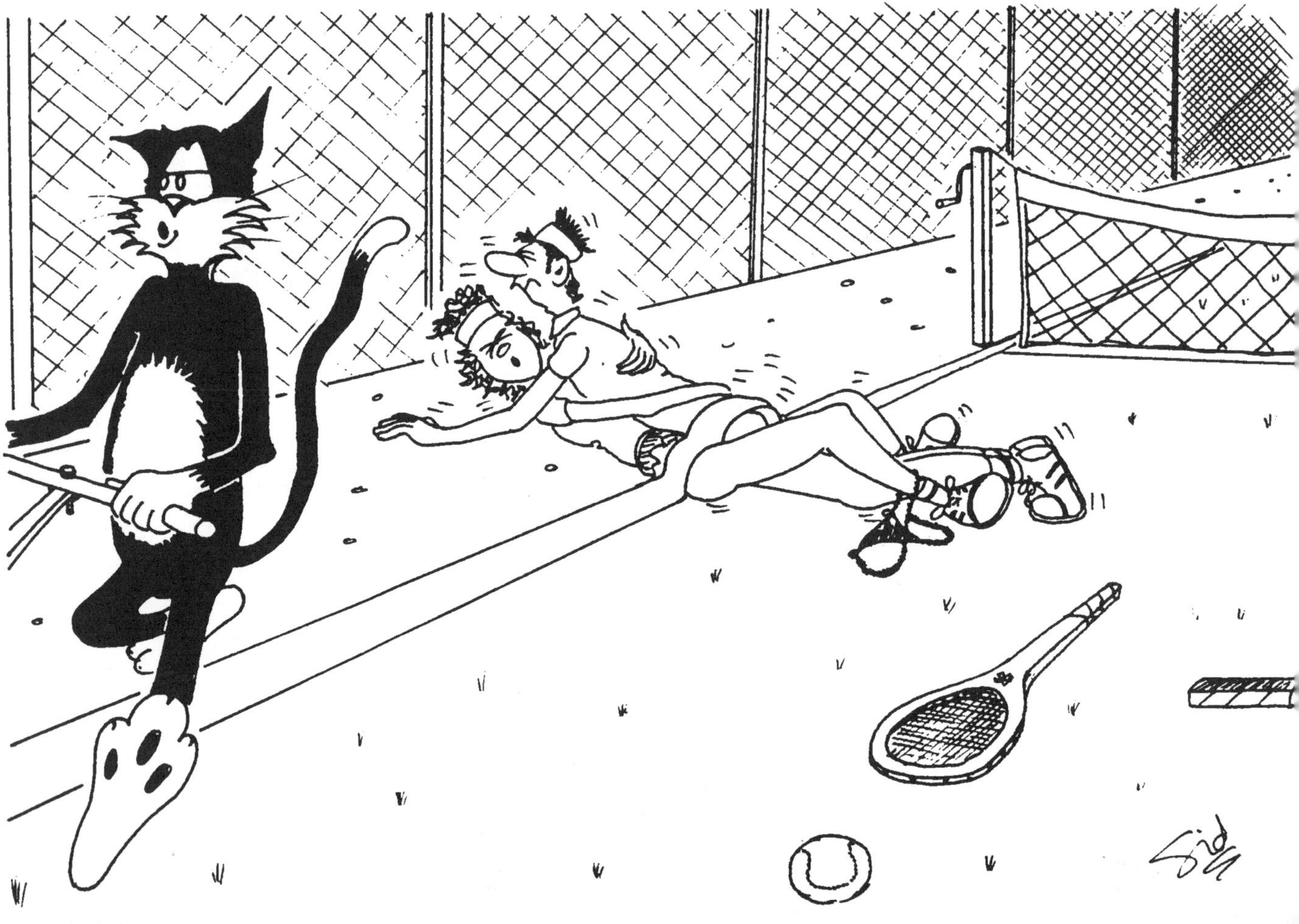

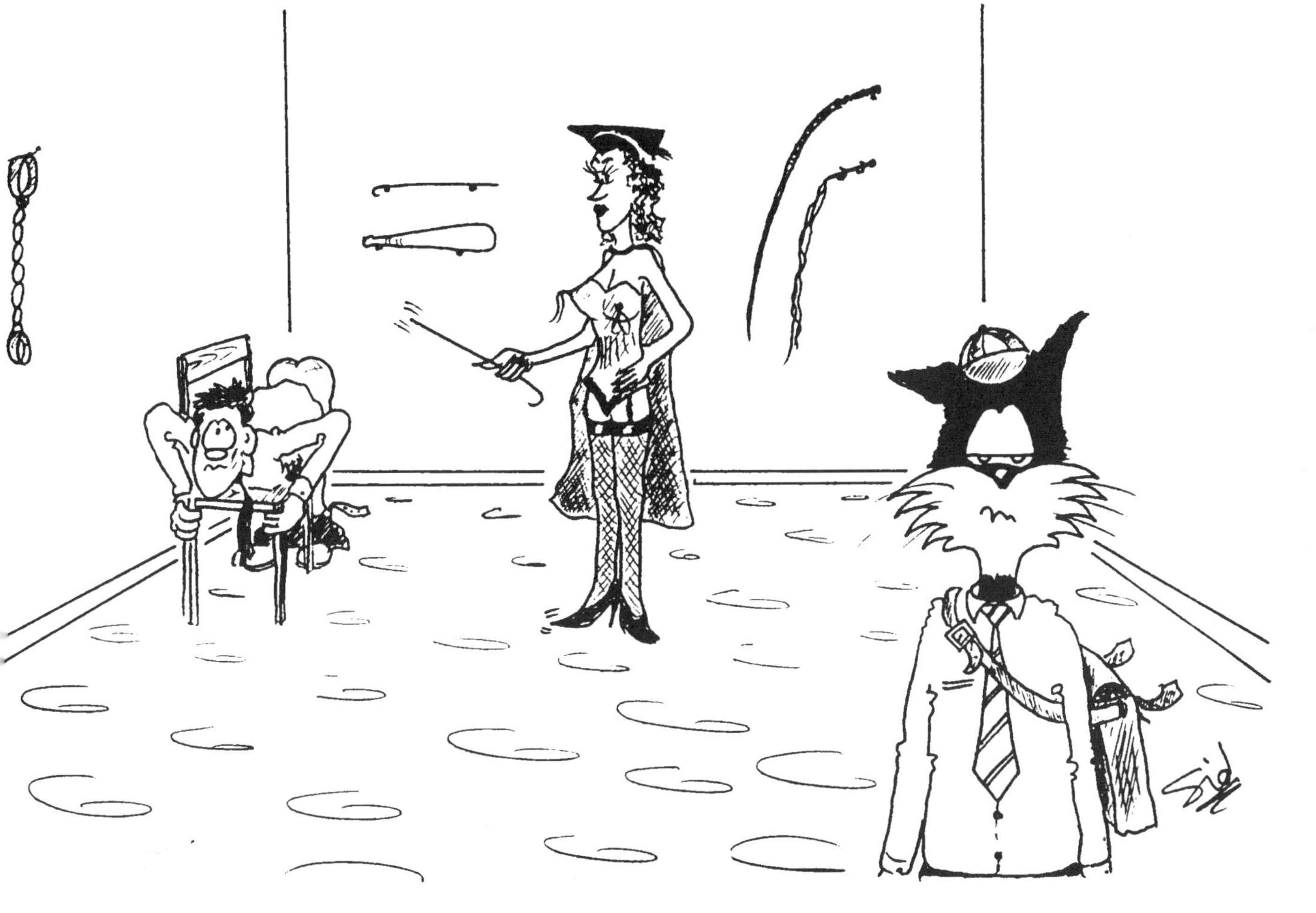
Sid

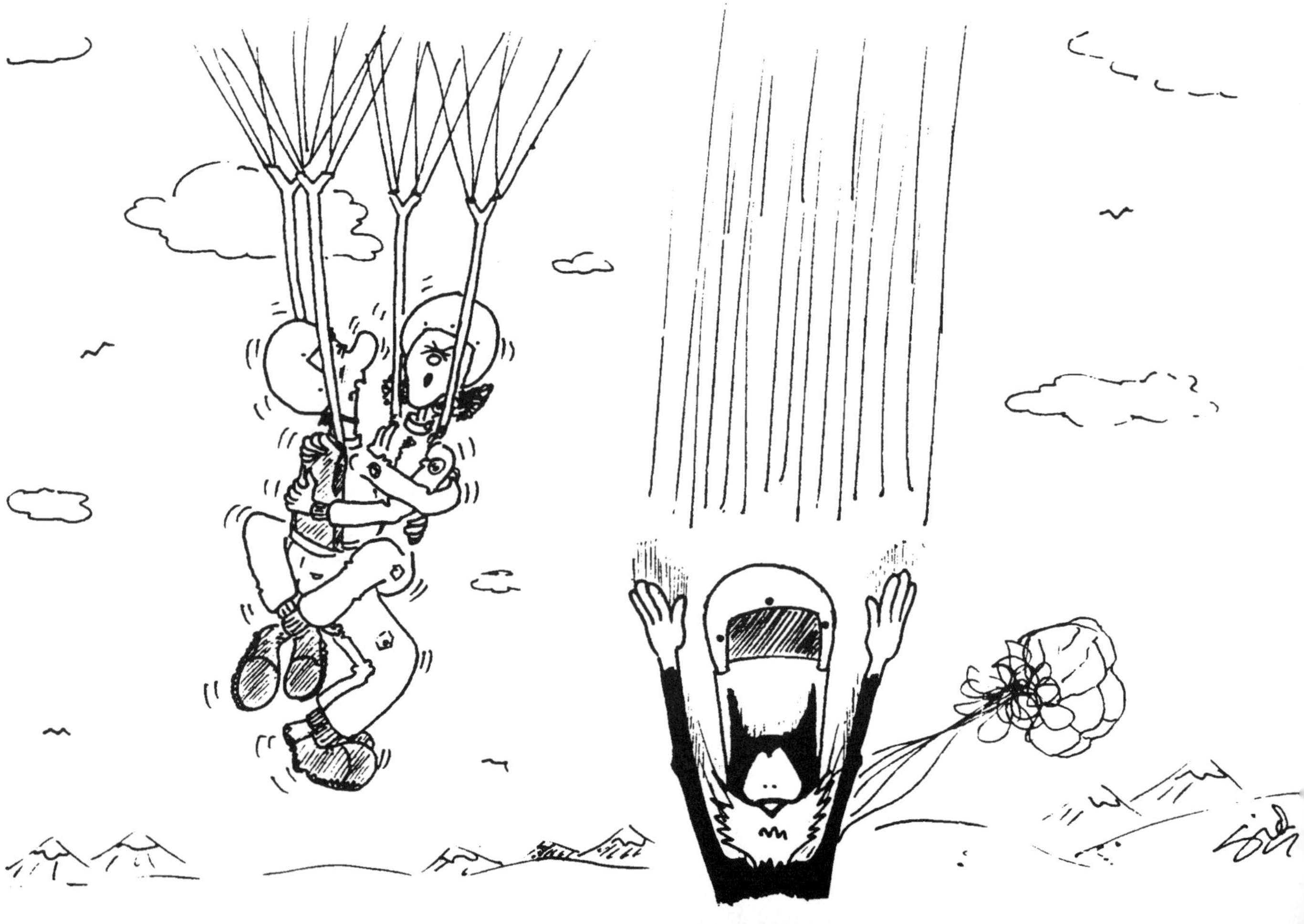

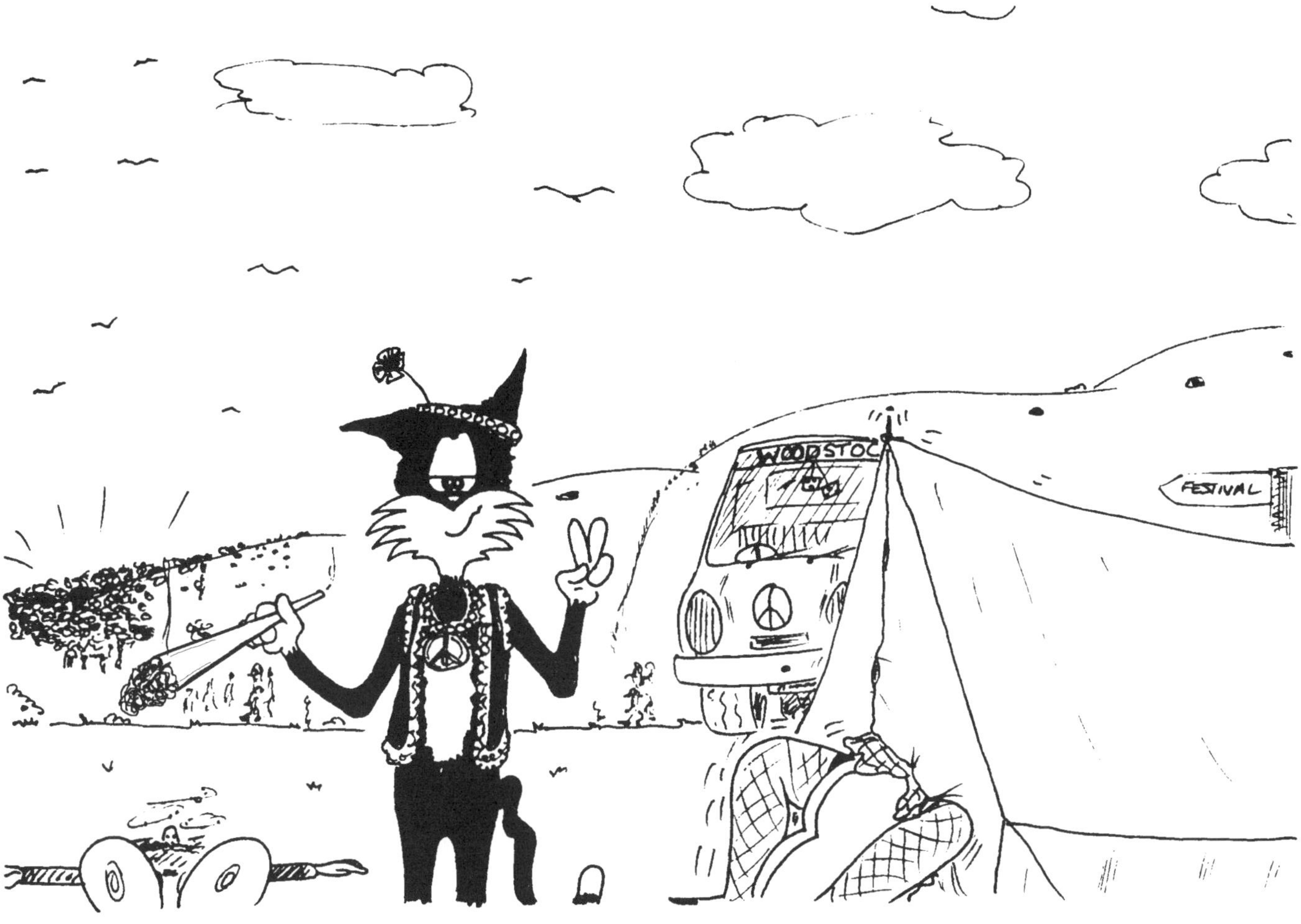

WOODSTOC
FESTIVAL

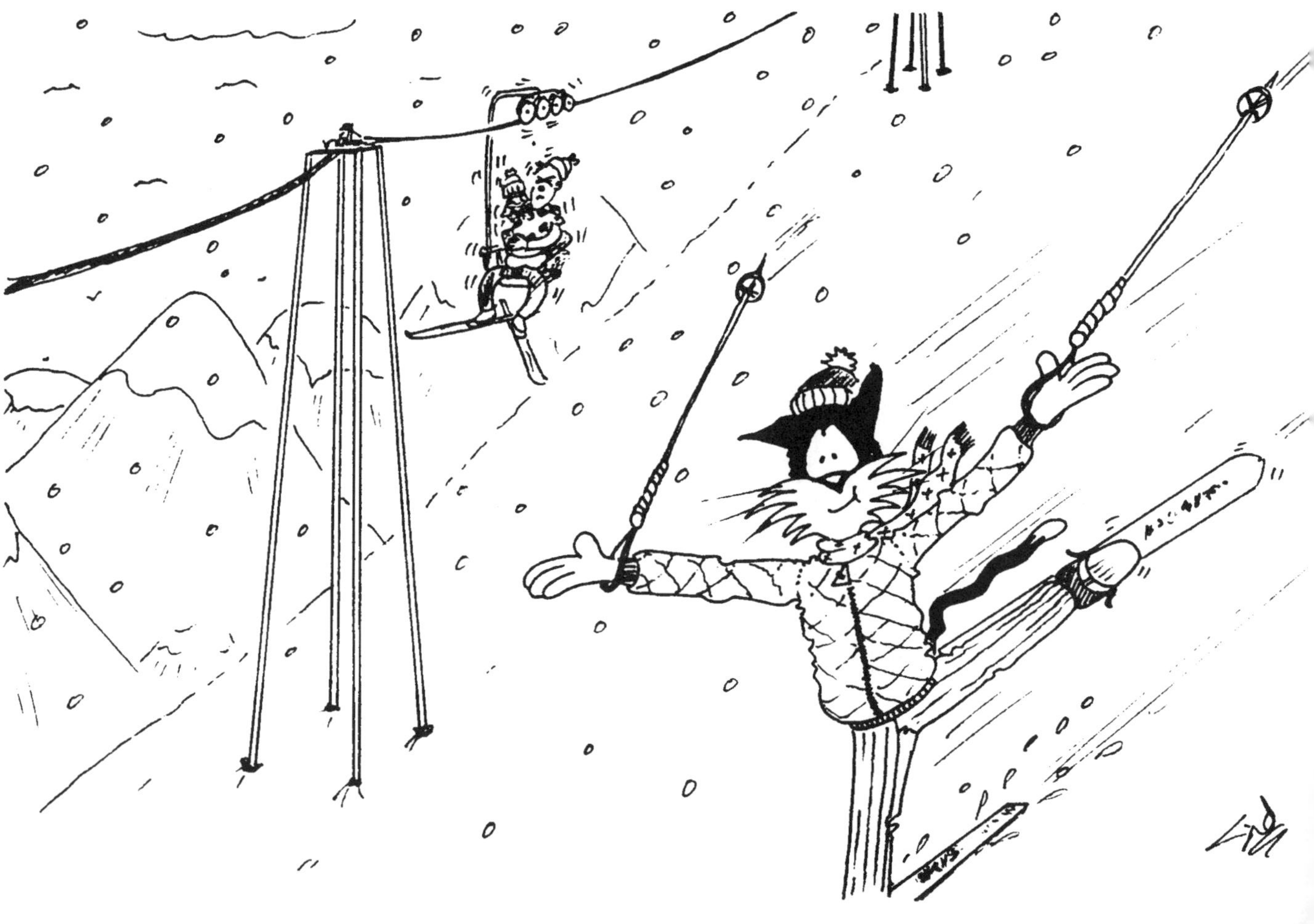

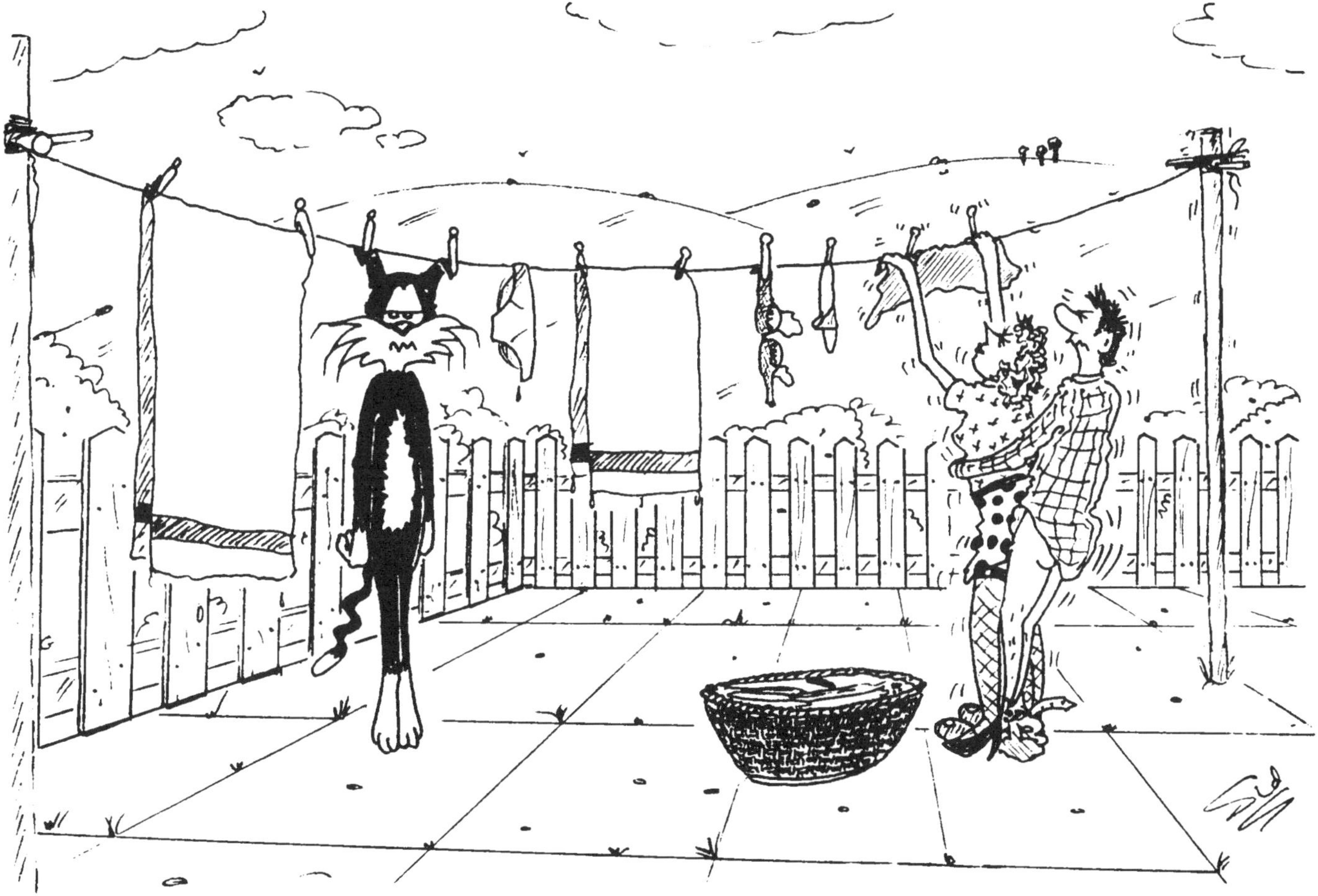

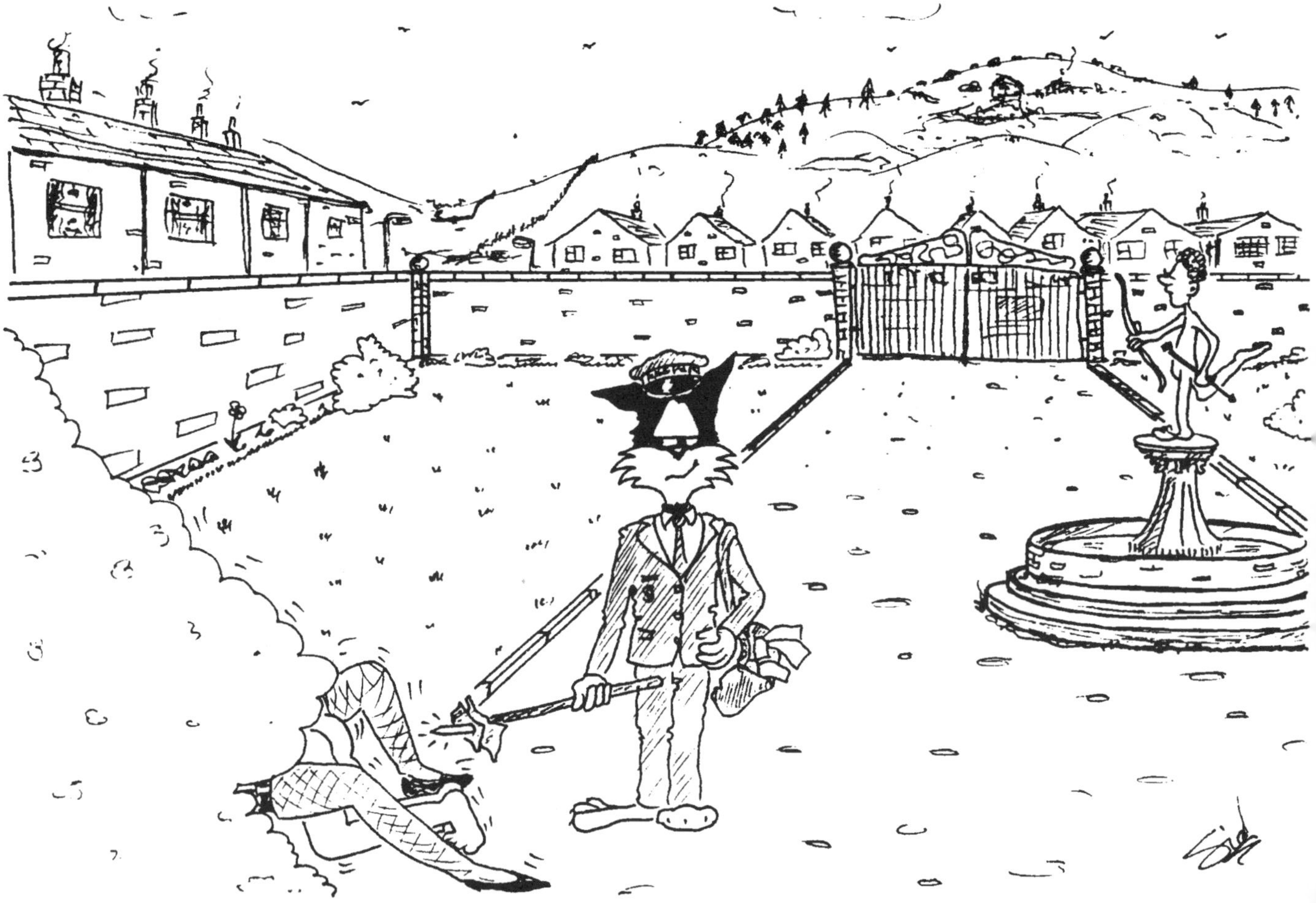

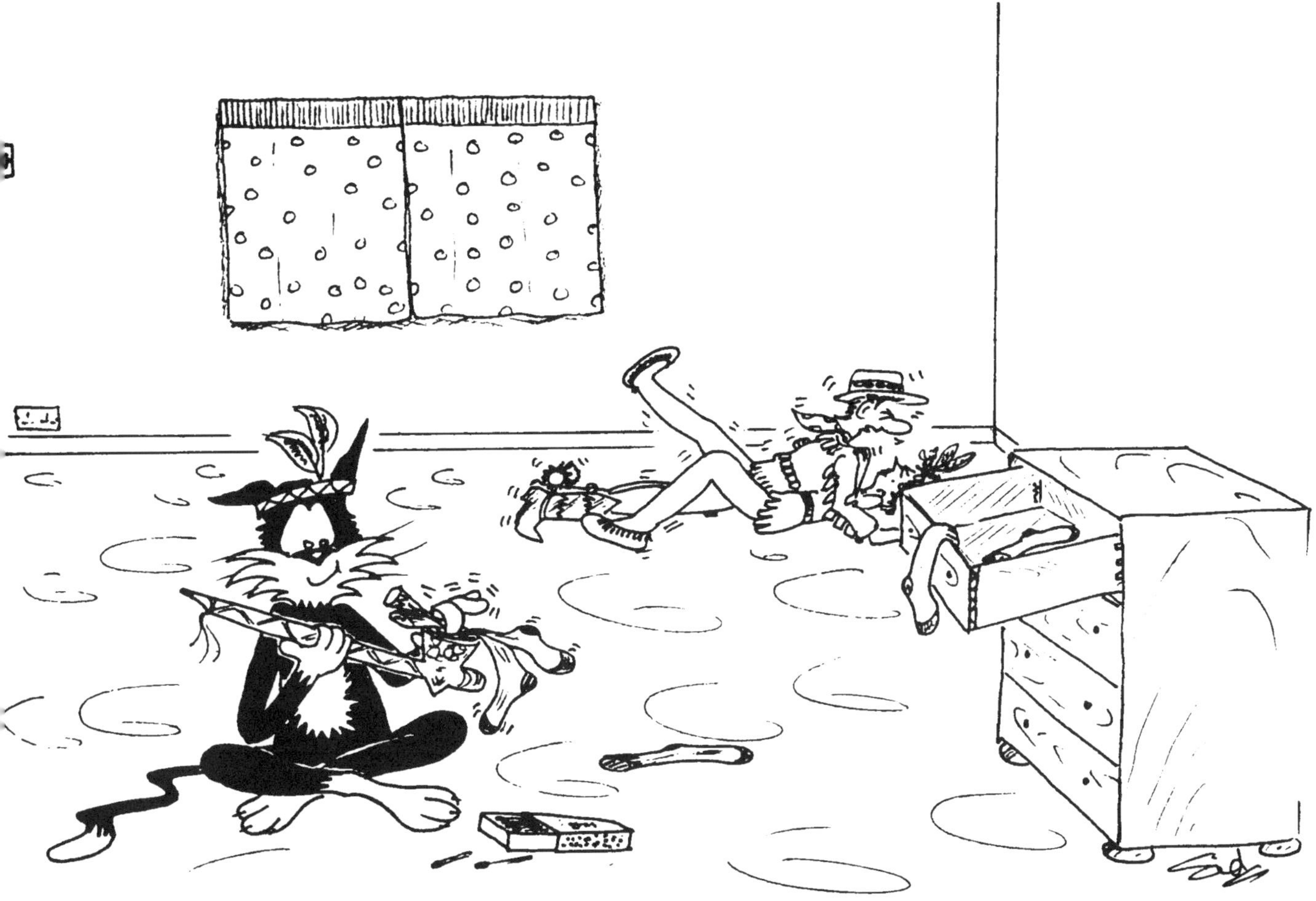

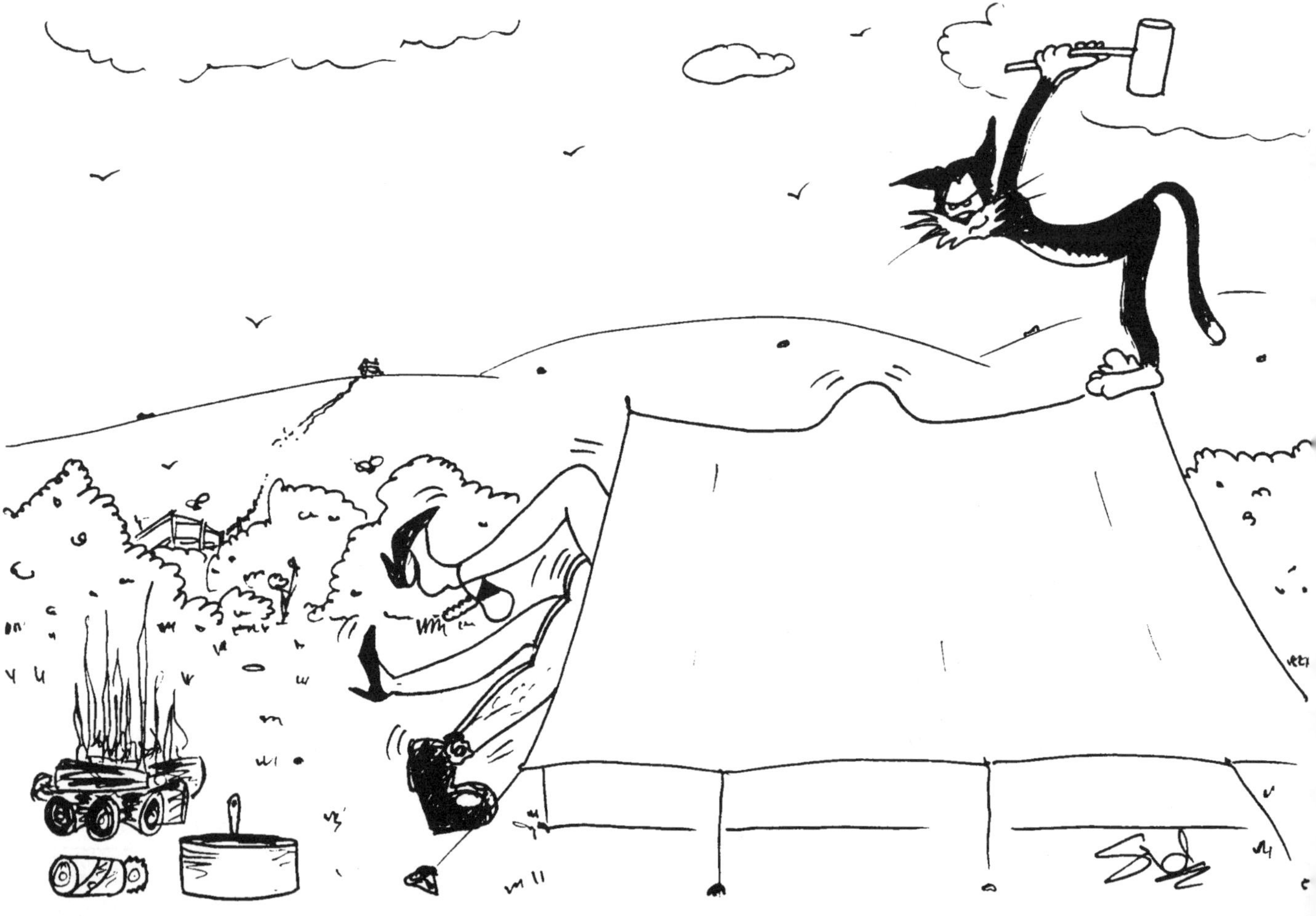

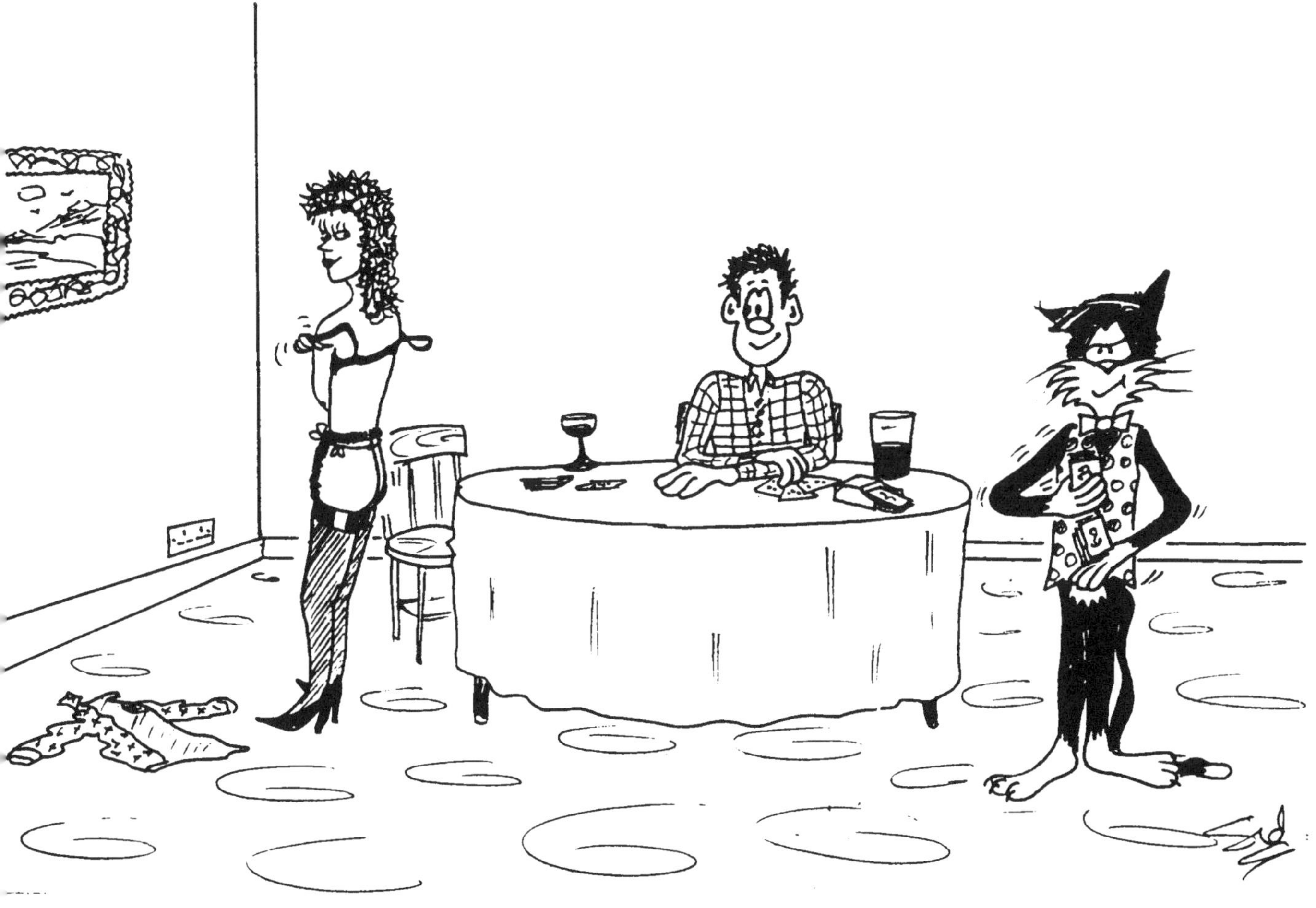

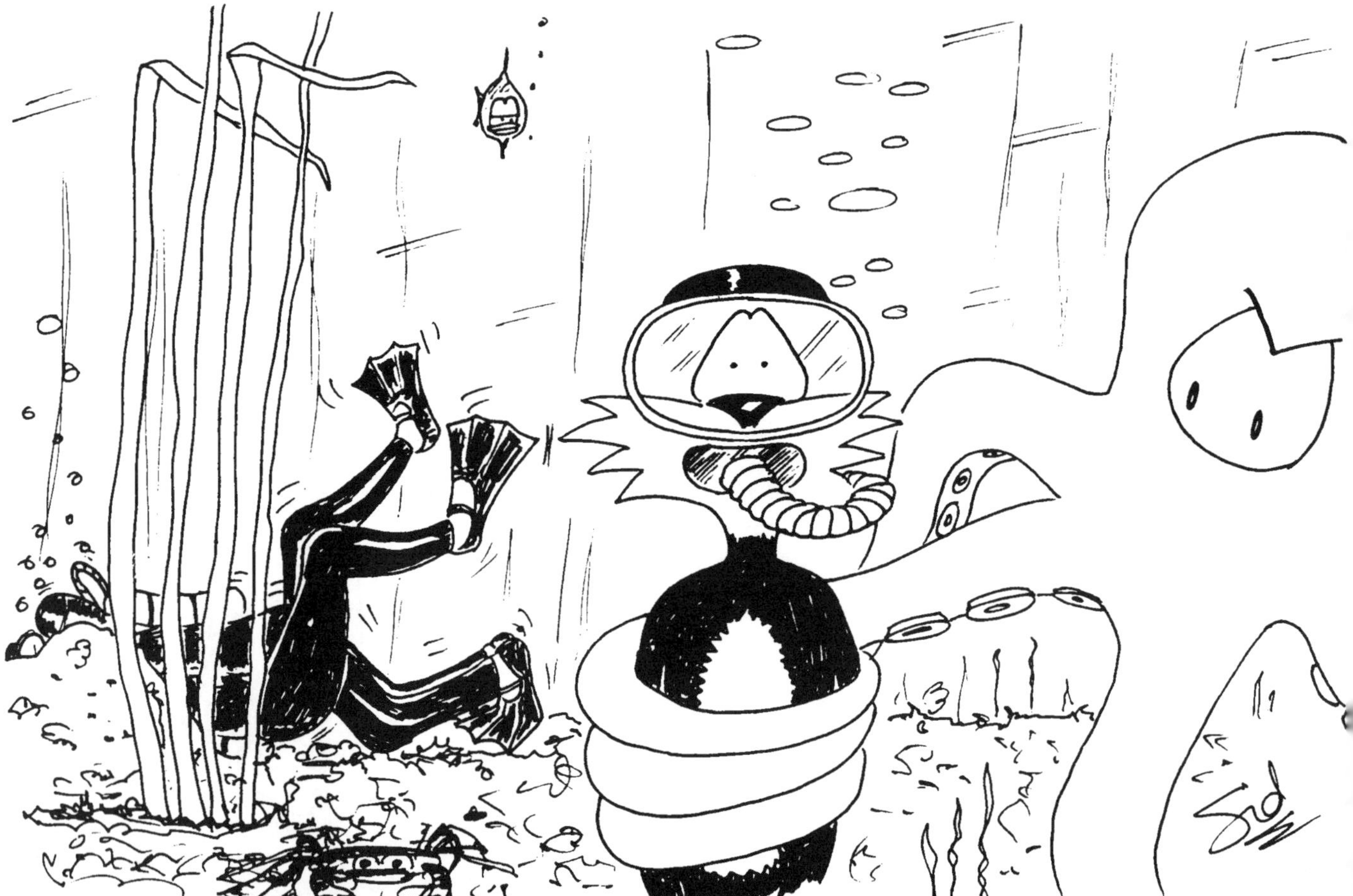

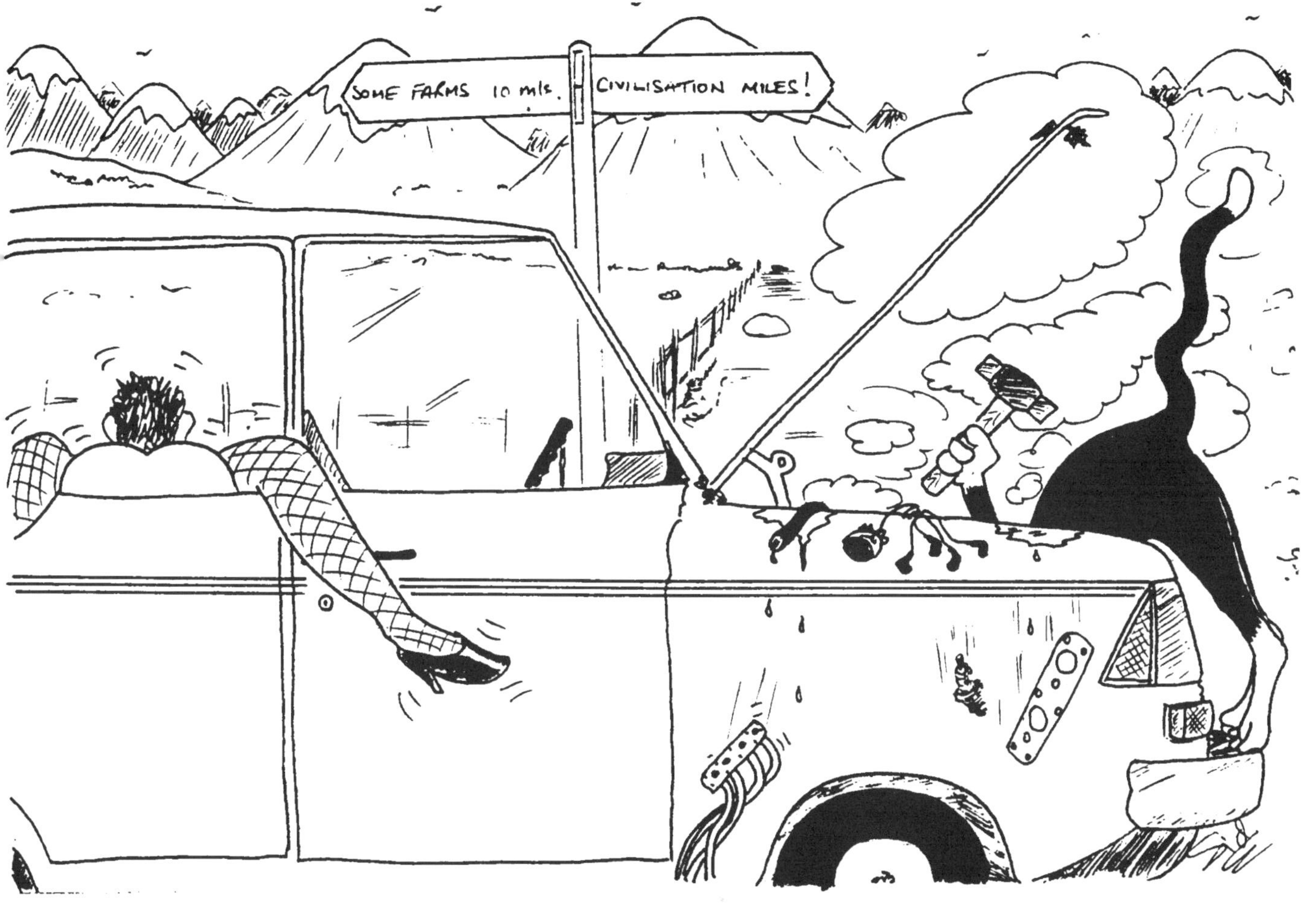
SOME FARMS 10 mls.
CIVILISATION MILES!

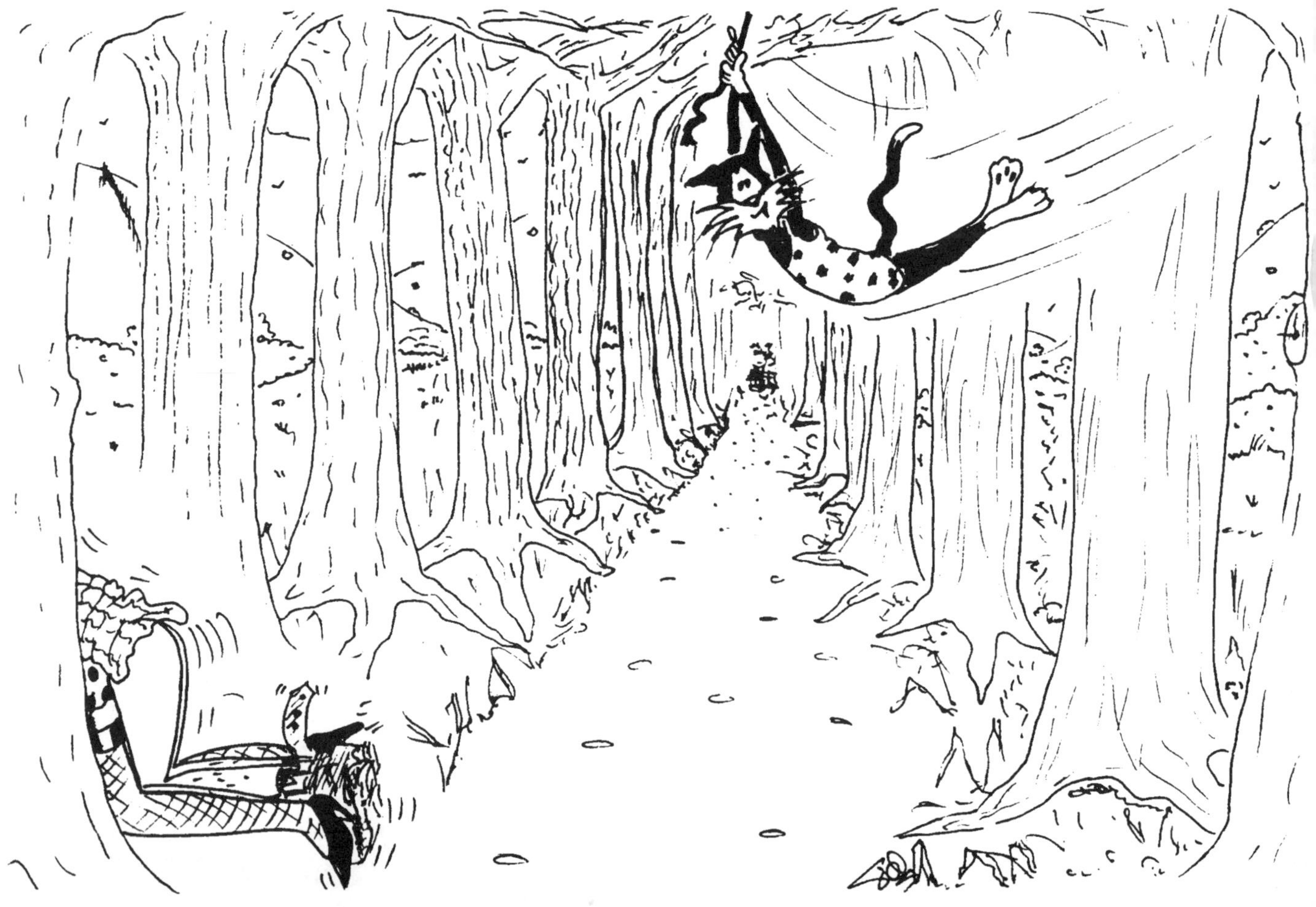

PHOTO BOOTH.
SNAPS HERE 5 MINS.
PASSPORTS, WALLETS OBCENETIES ETC.
75p.

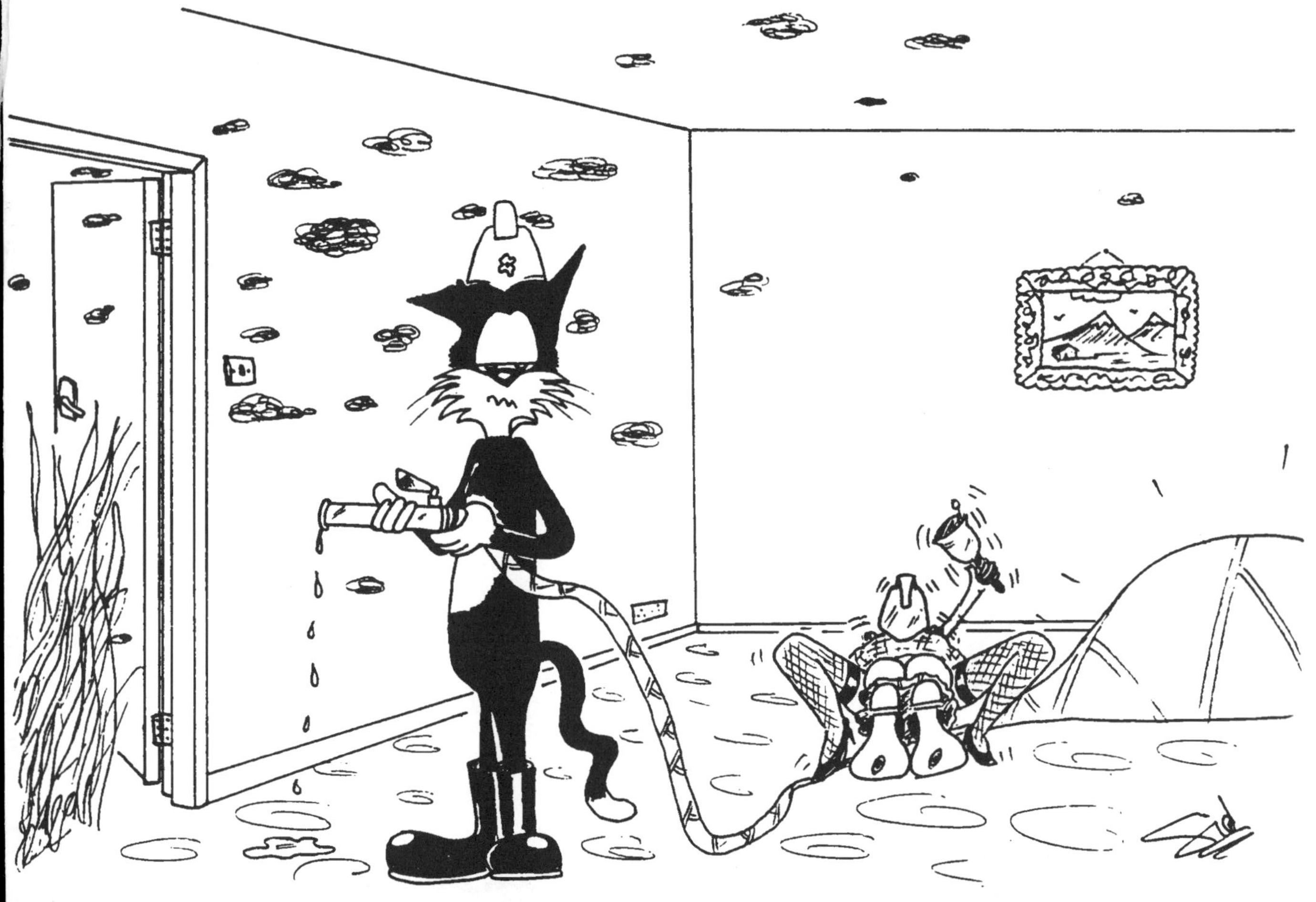

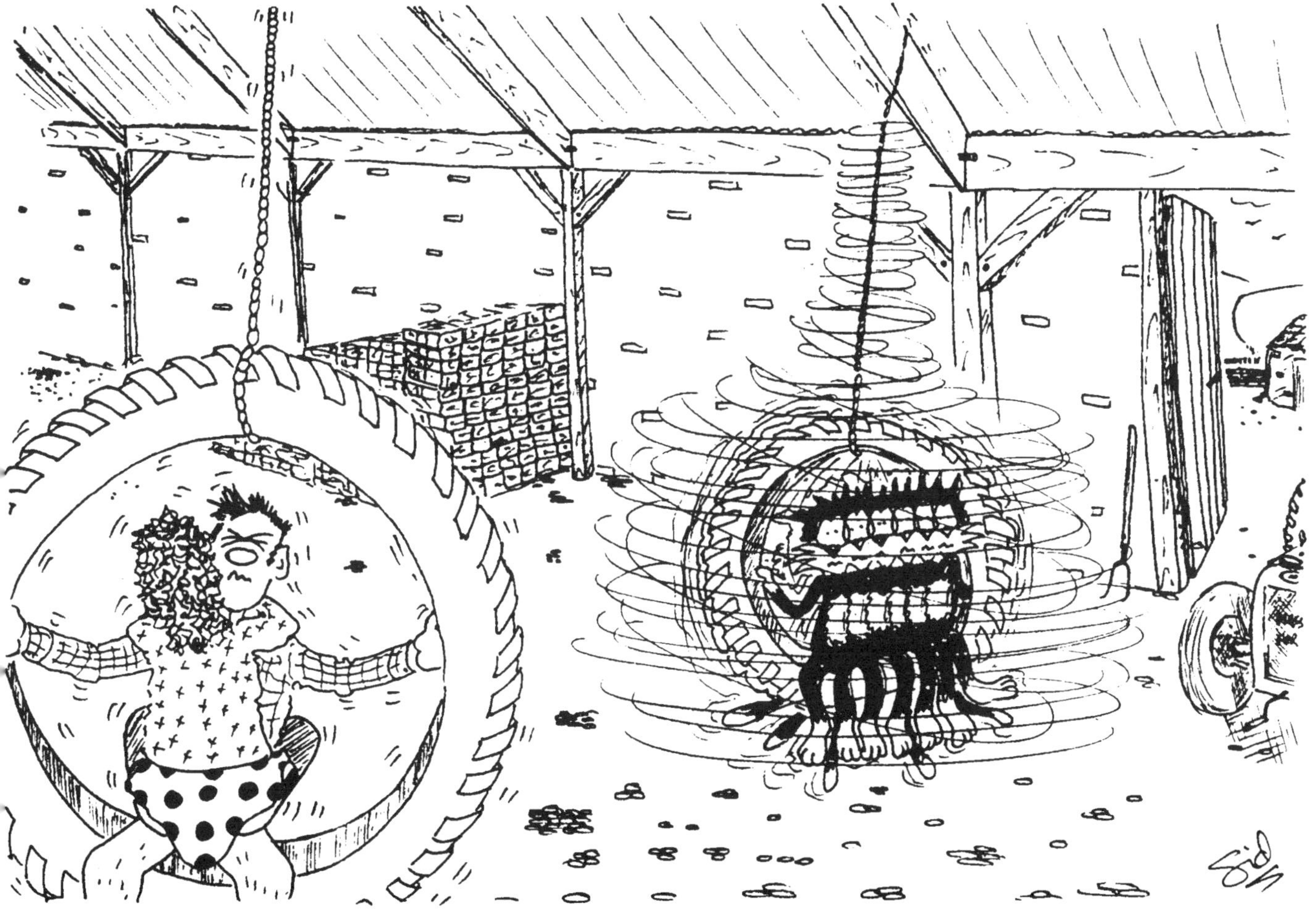
Sid

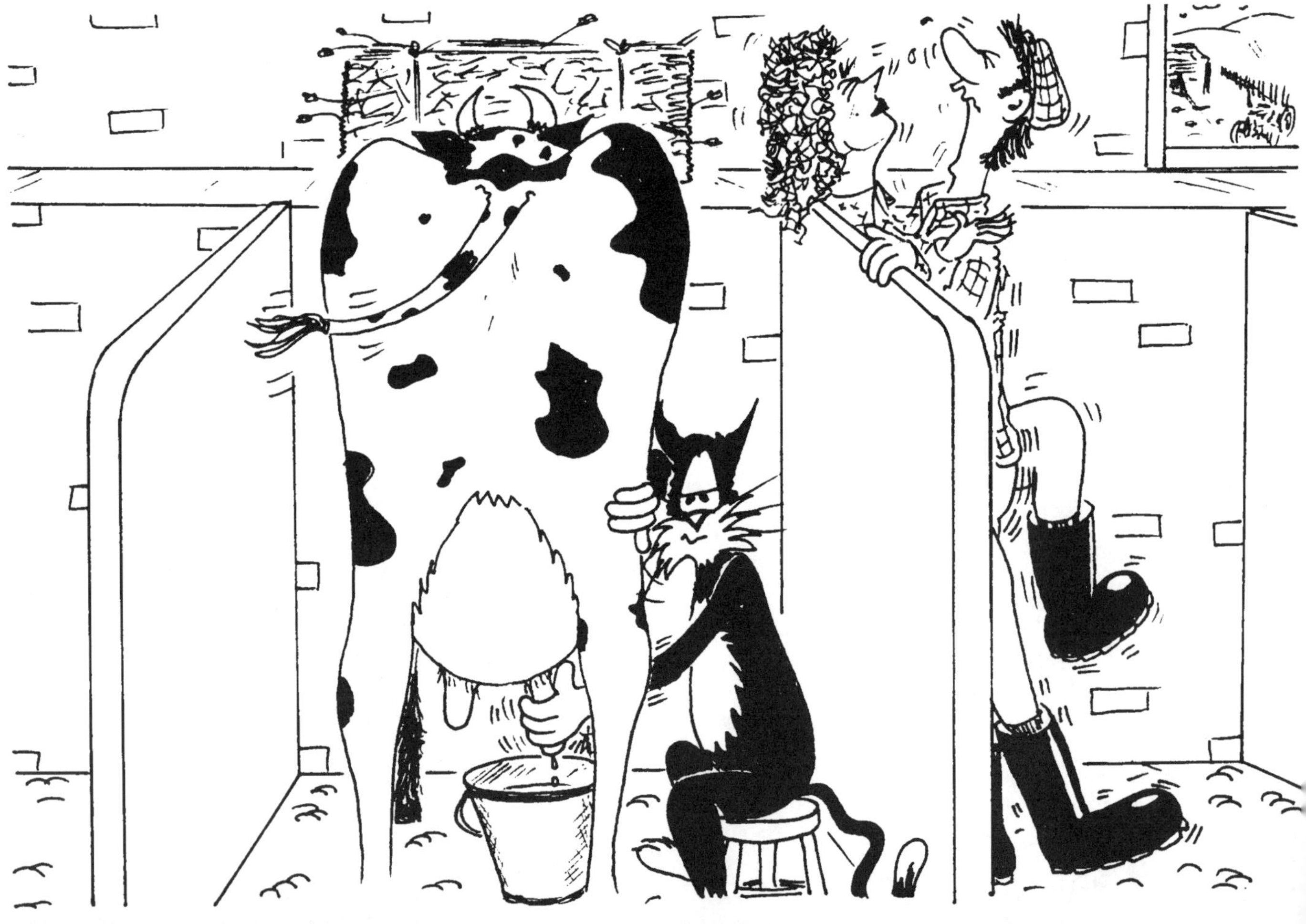

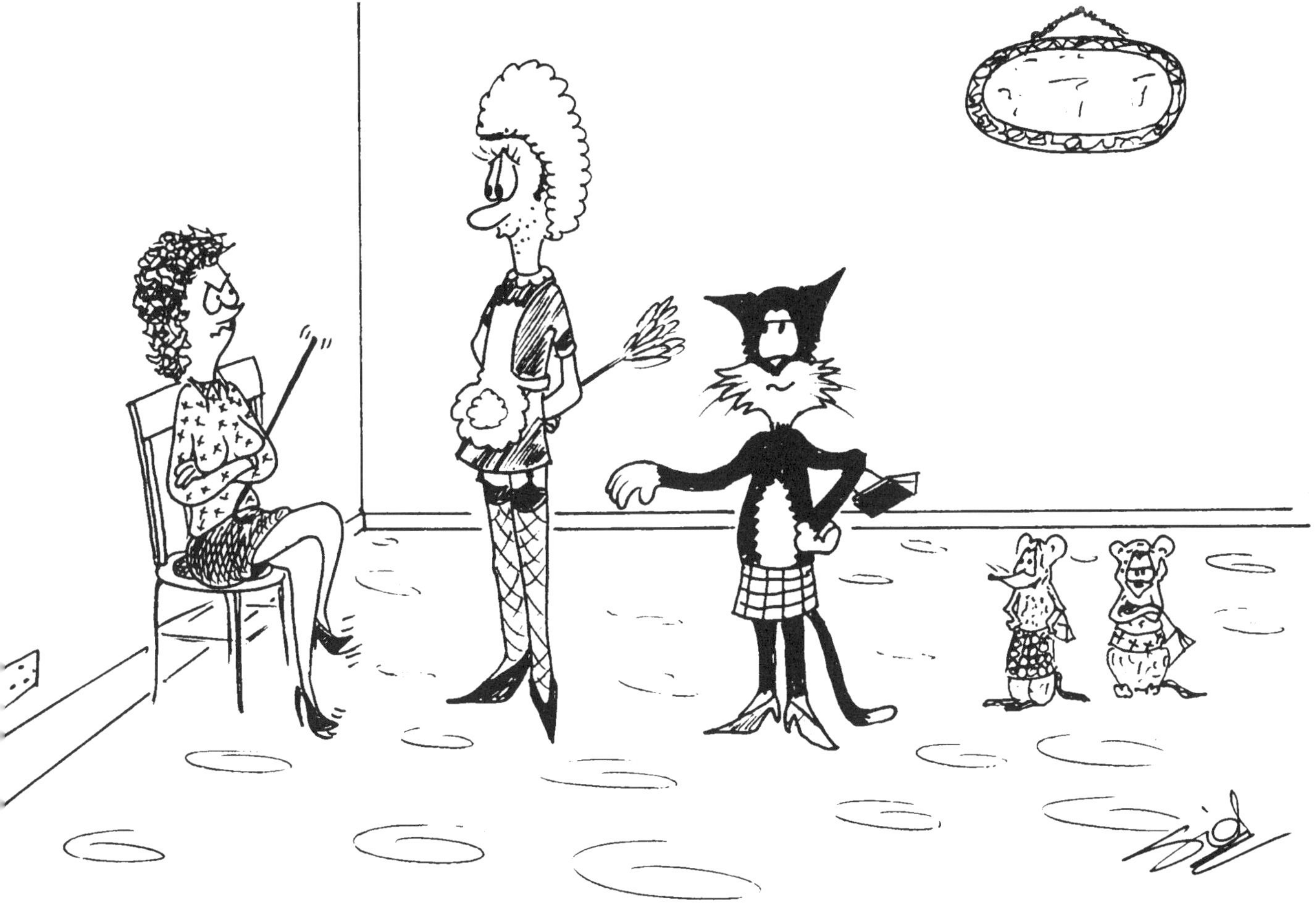
Sid

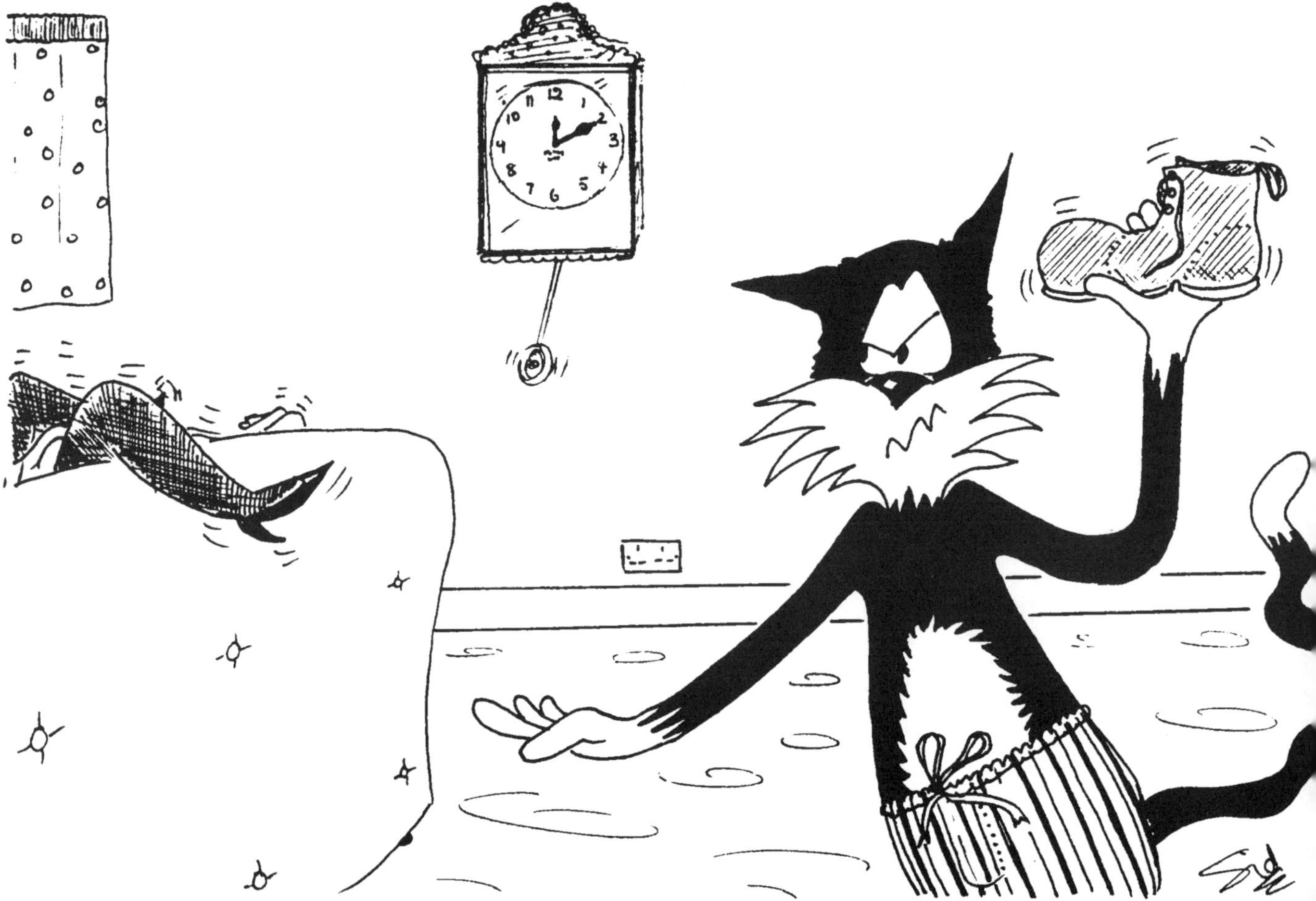

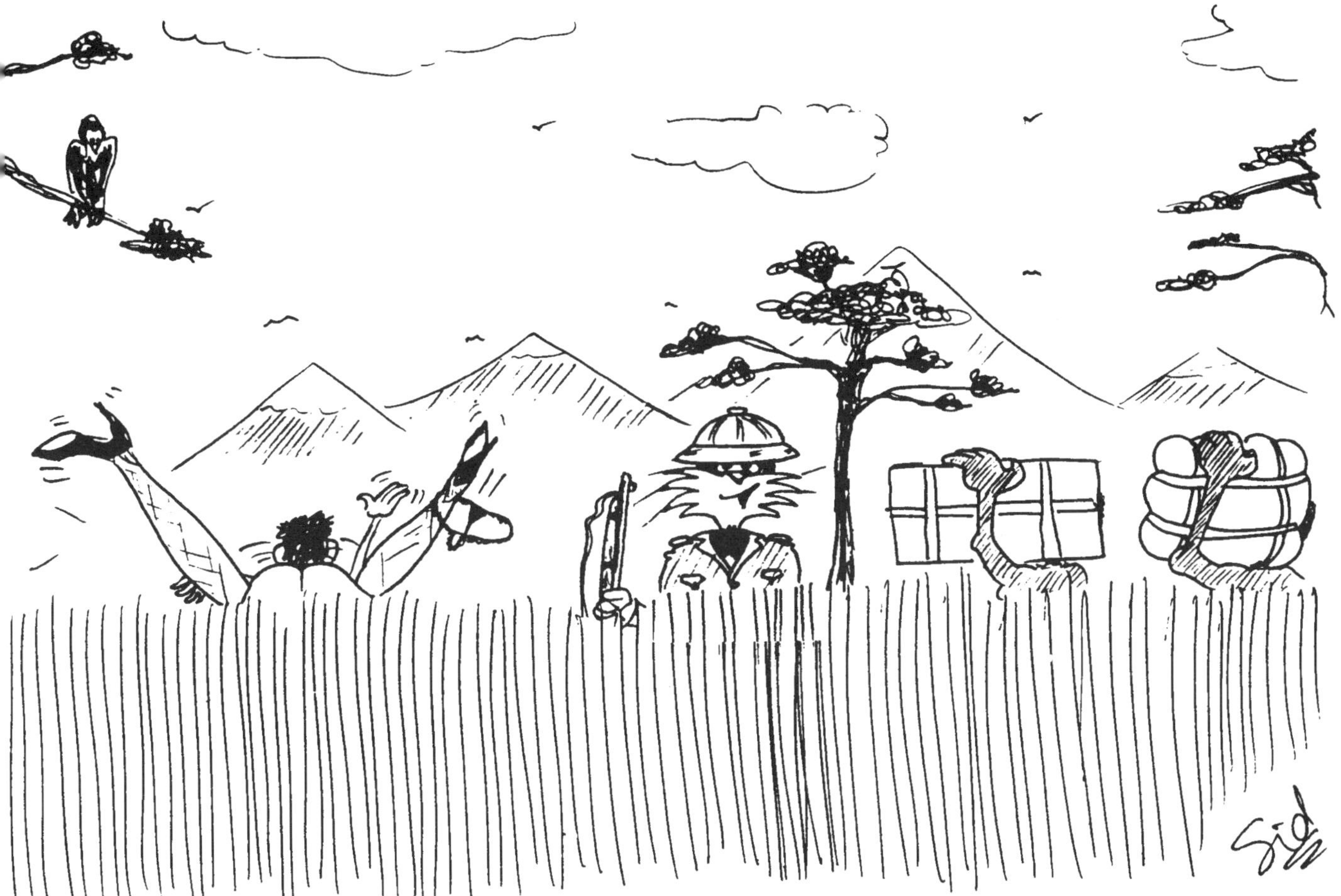
Sid

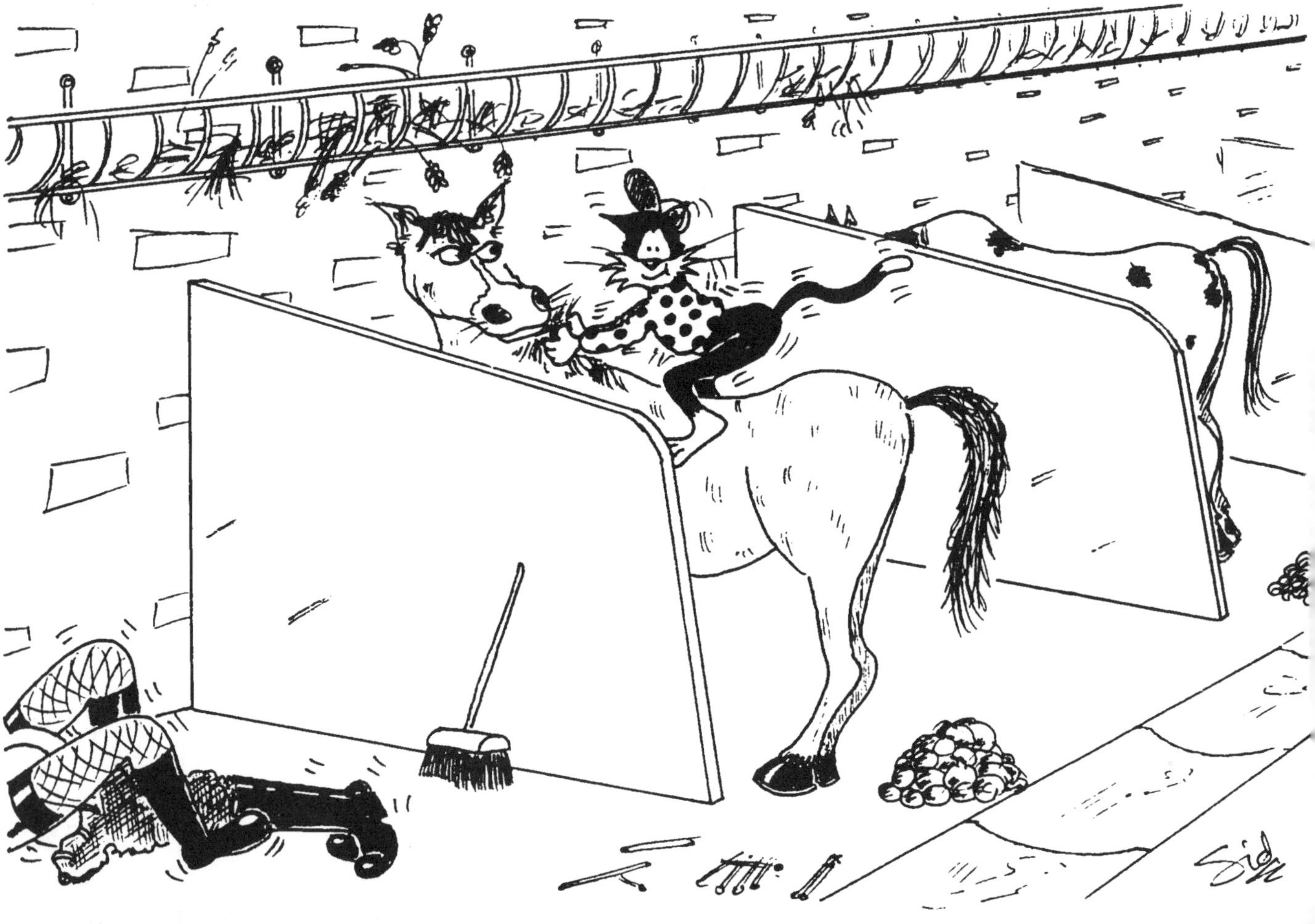
Sid

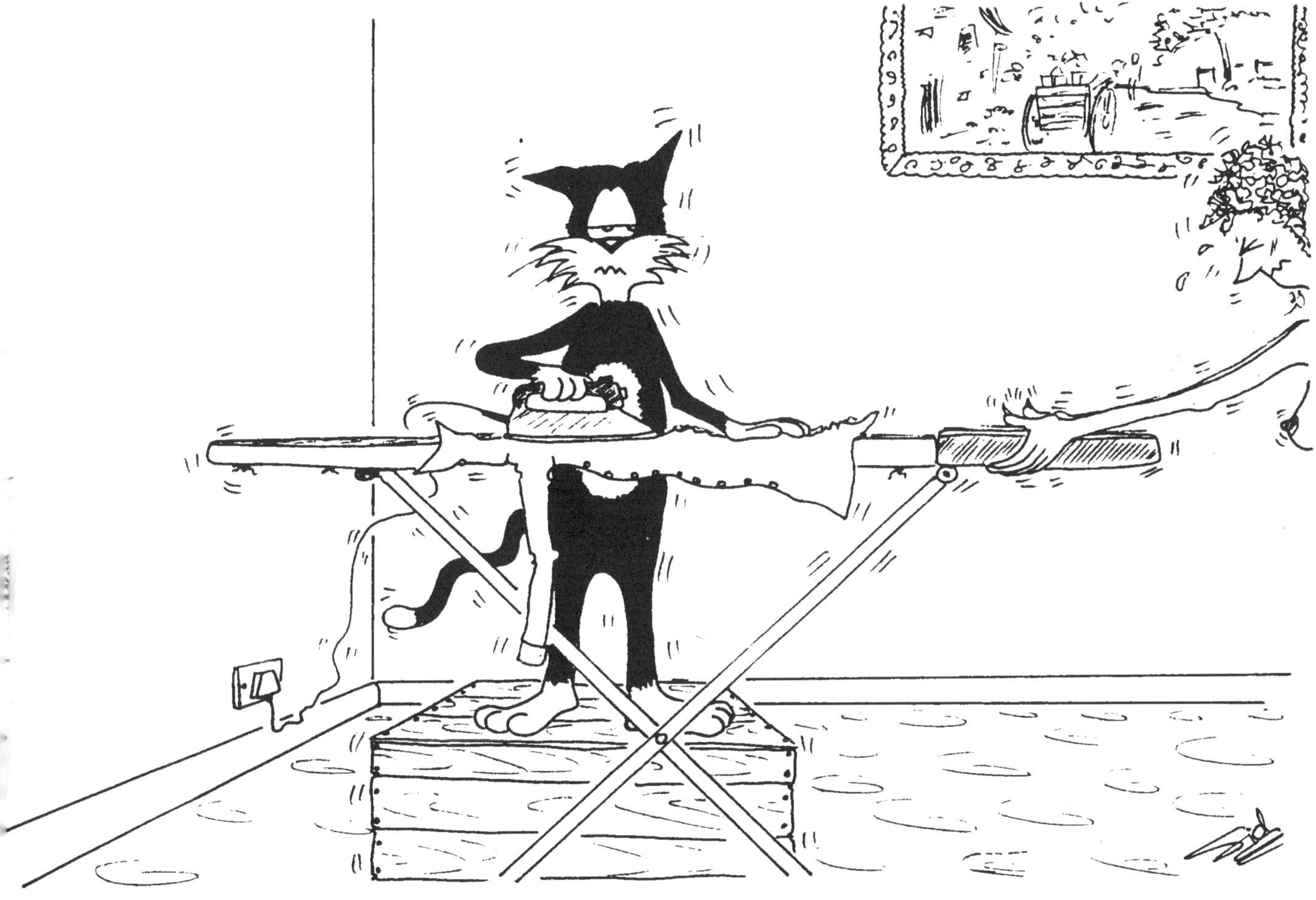

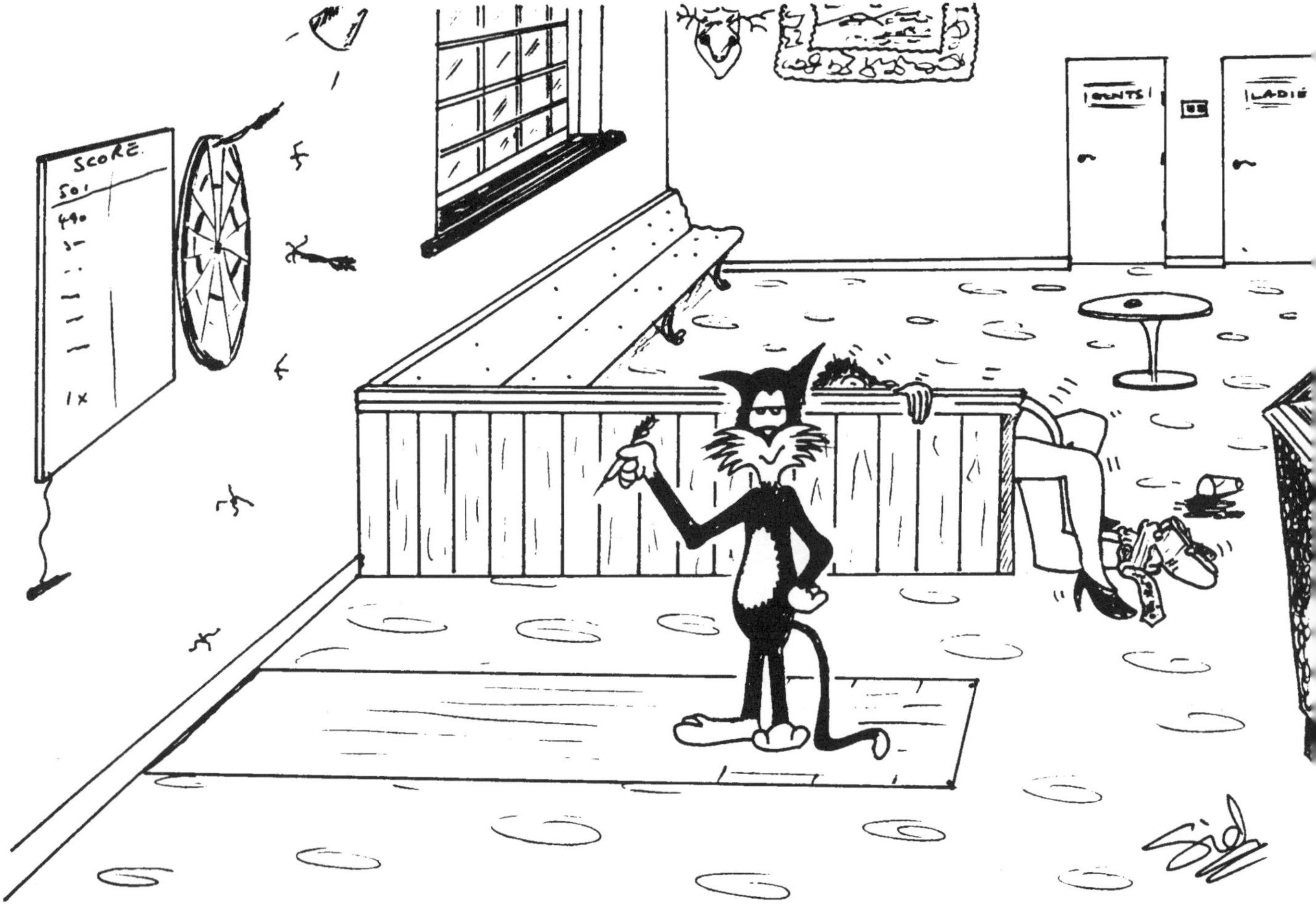
SCORE
501
1x

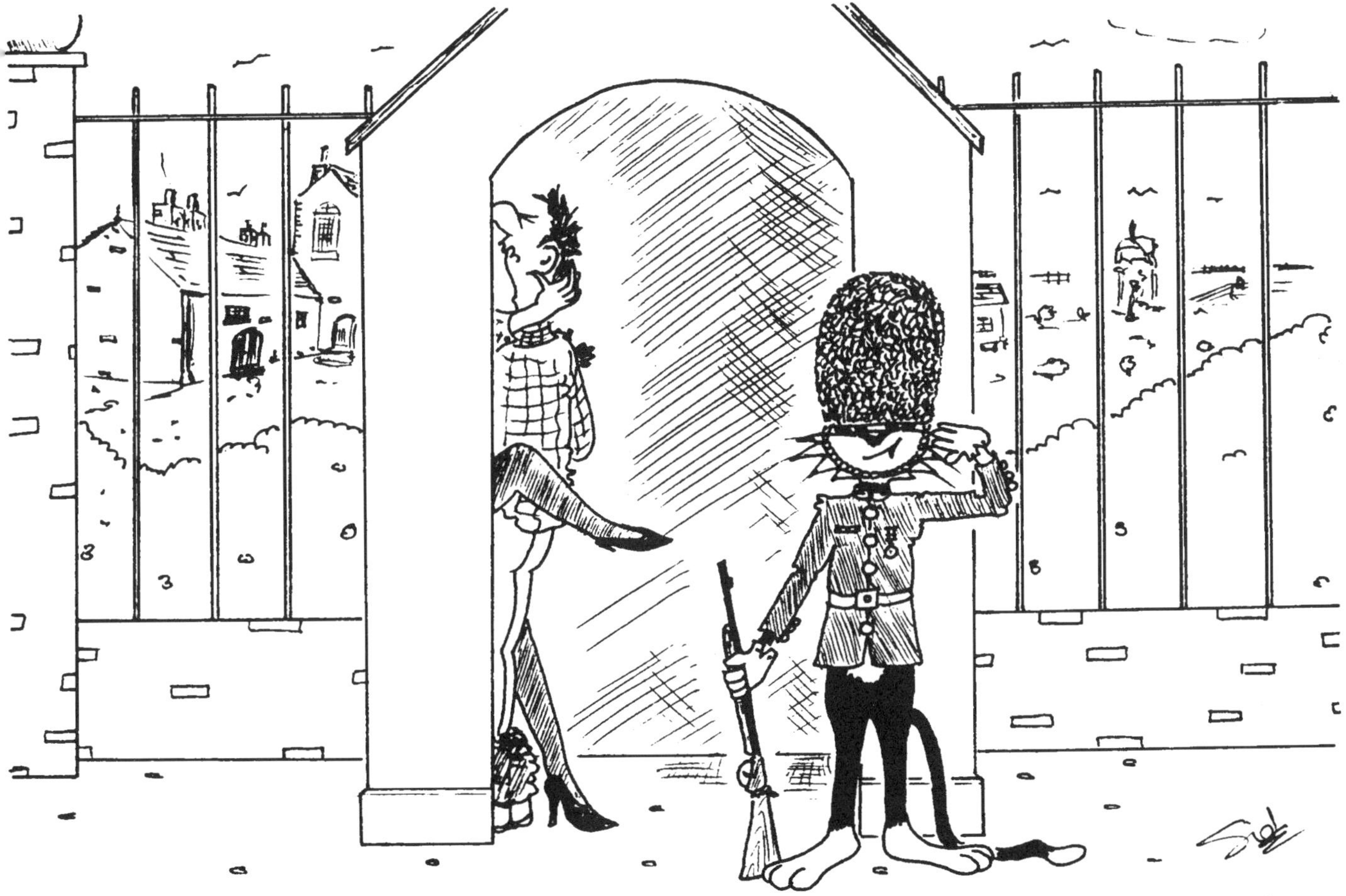

SPECIAL
FROZEN PEAS
LOW LOW
BIG
CRISP FLAKES
SUPER CAT
SAGE + ONION STUFFING
ECONOMY FLOUR
TEA BAGS
TEA BAGS
CAT
CORN
BRAN
Sid

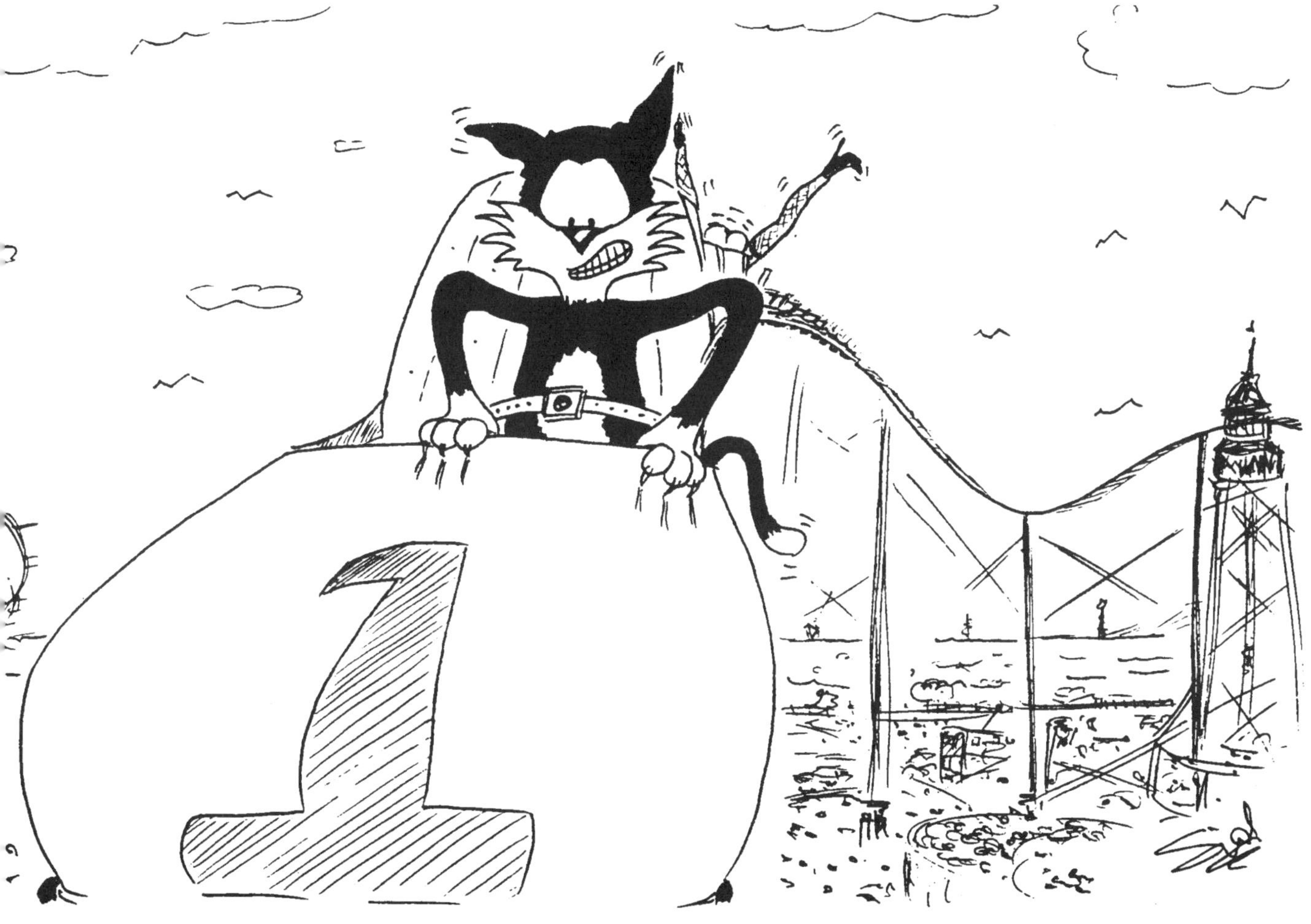

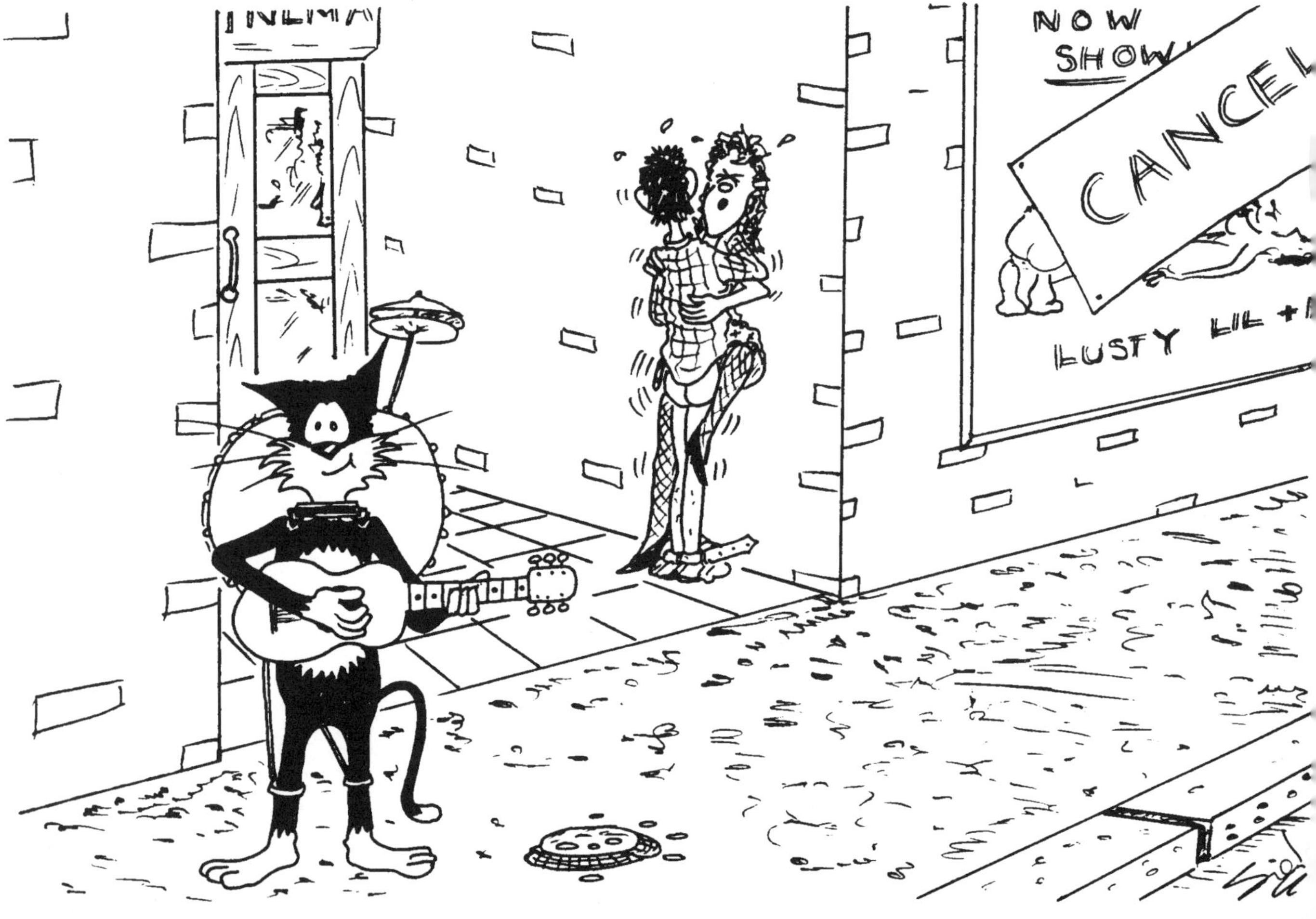
NOW
SHOW
CANCEL
LUSTY LIL

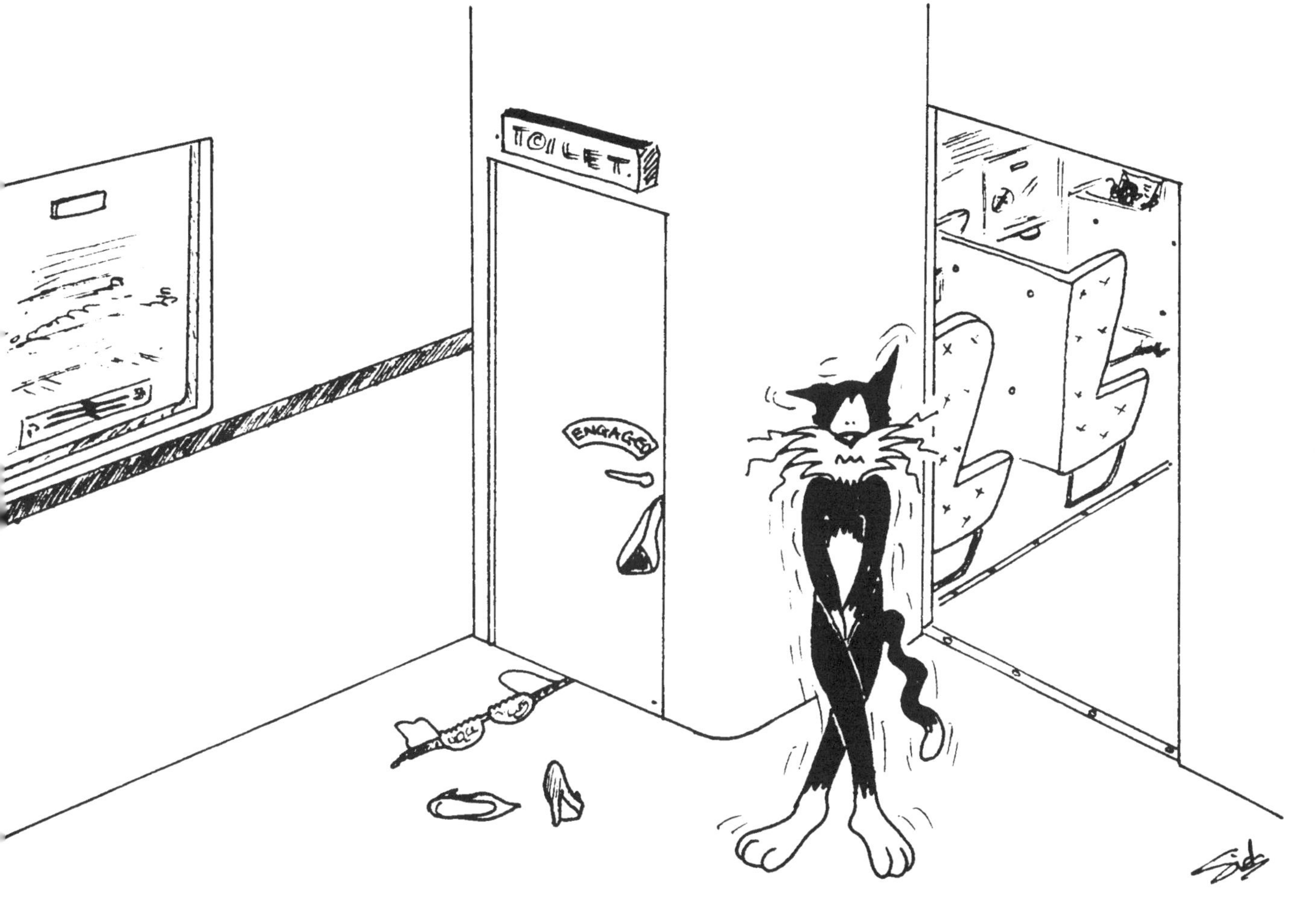
TOILET.
ENGAGED

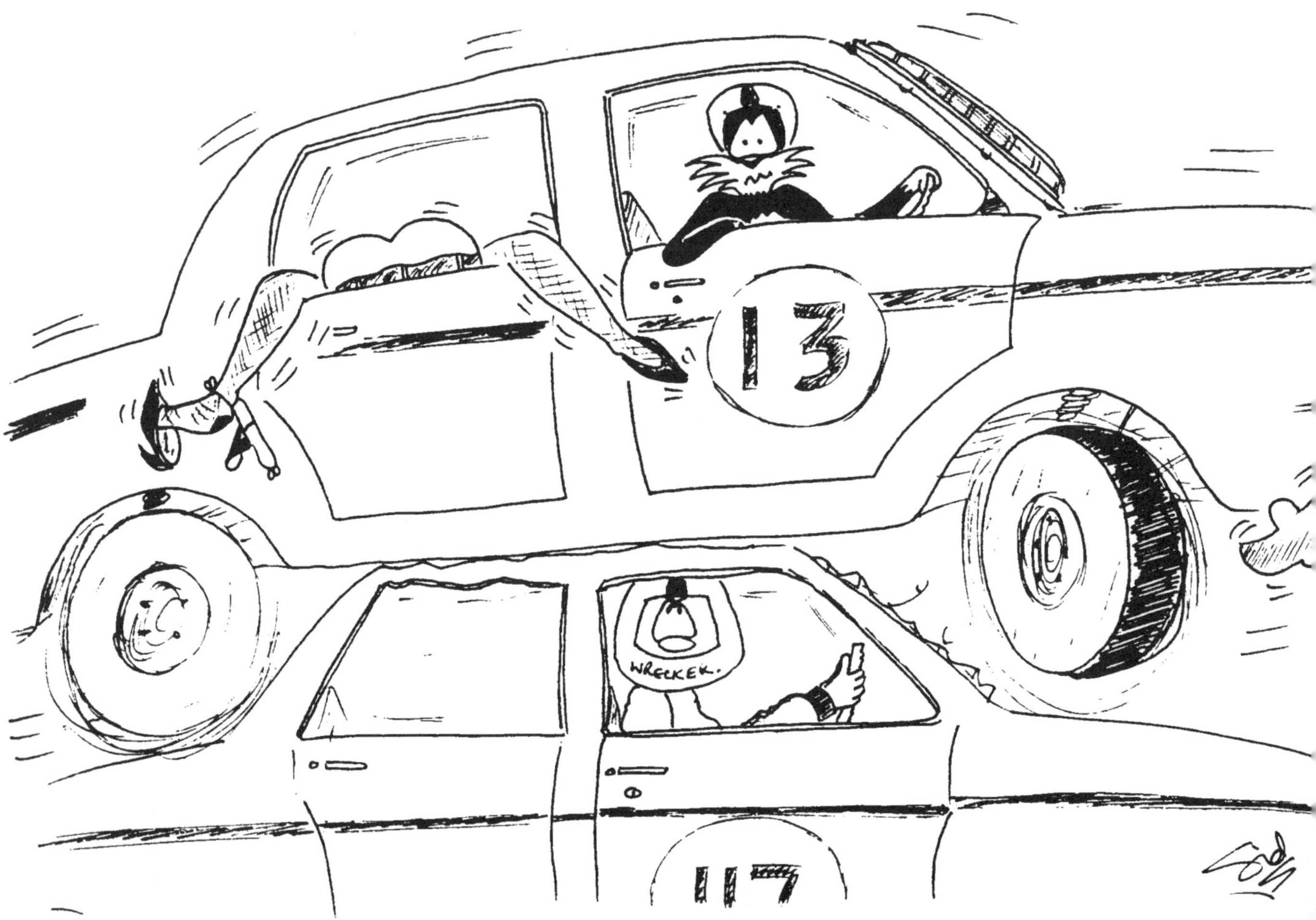
13
WRECKER.
117

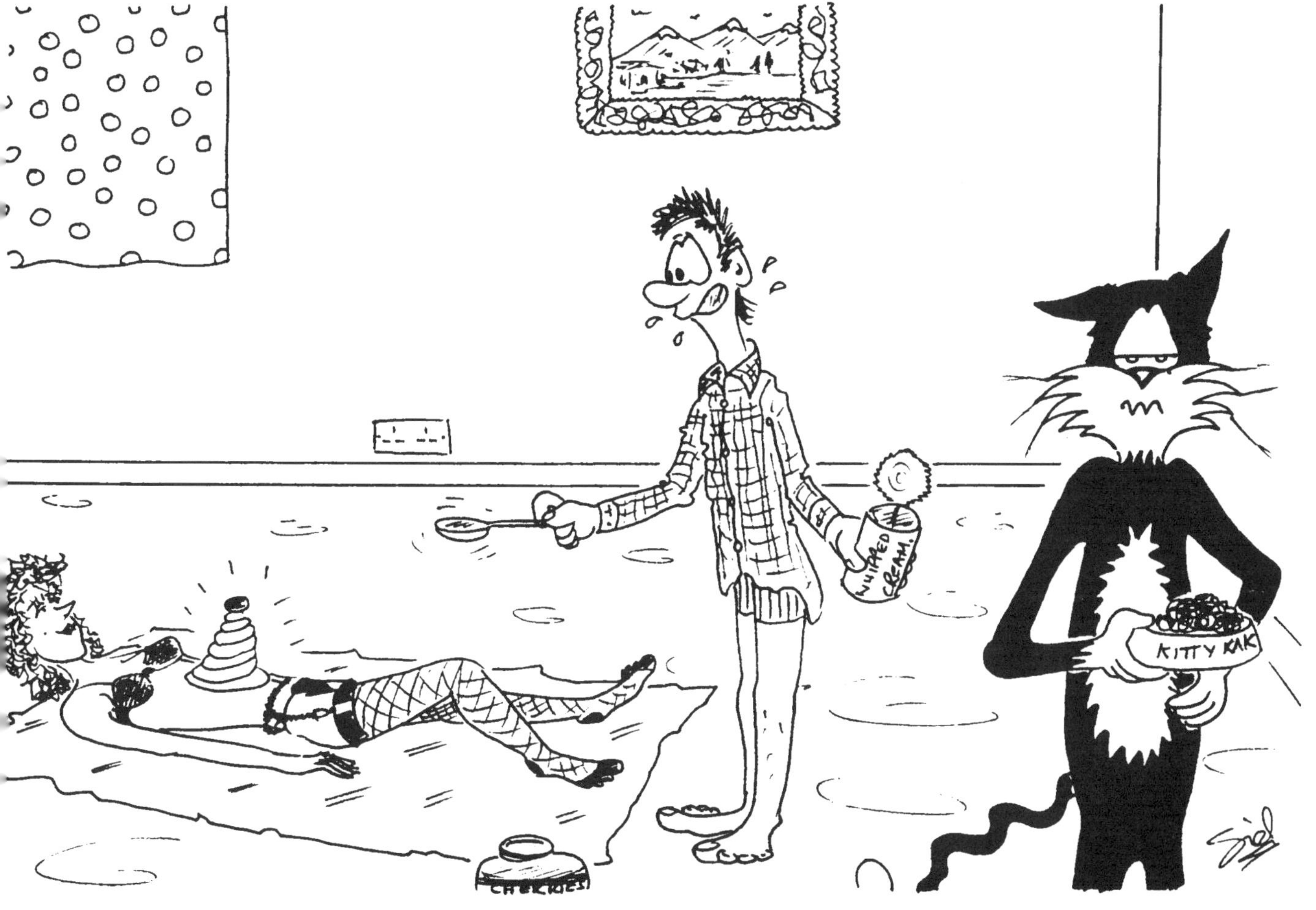
WHIPPED CREAM.
KITTY KAK
CHERRIES

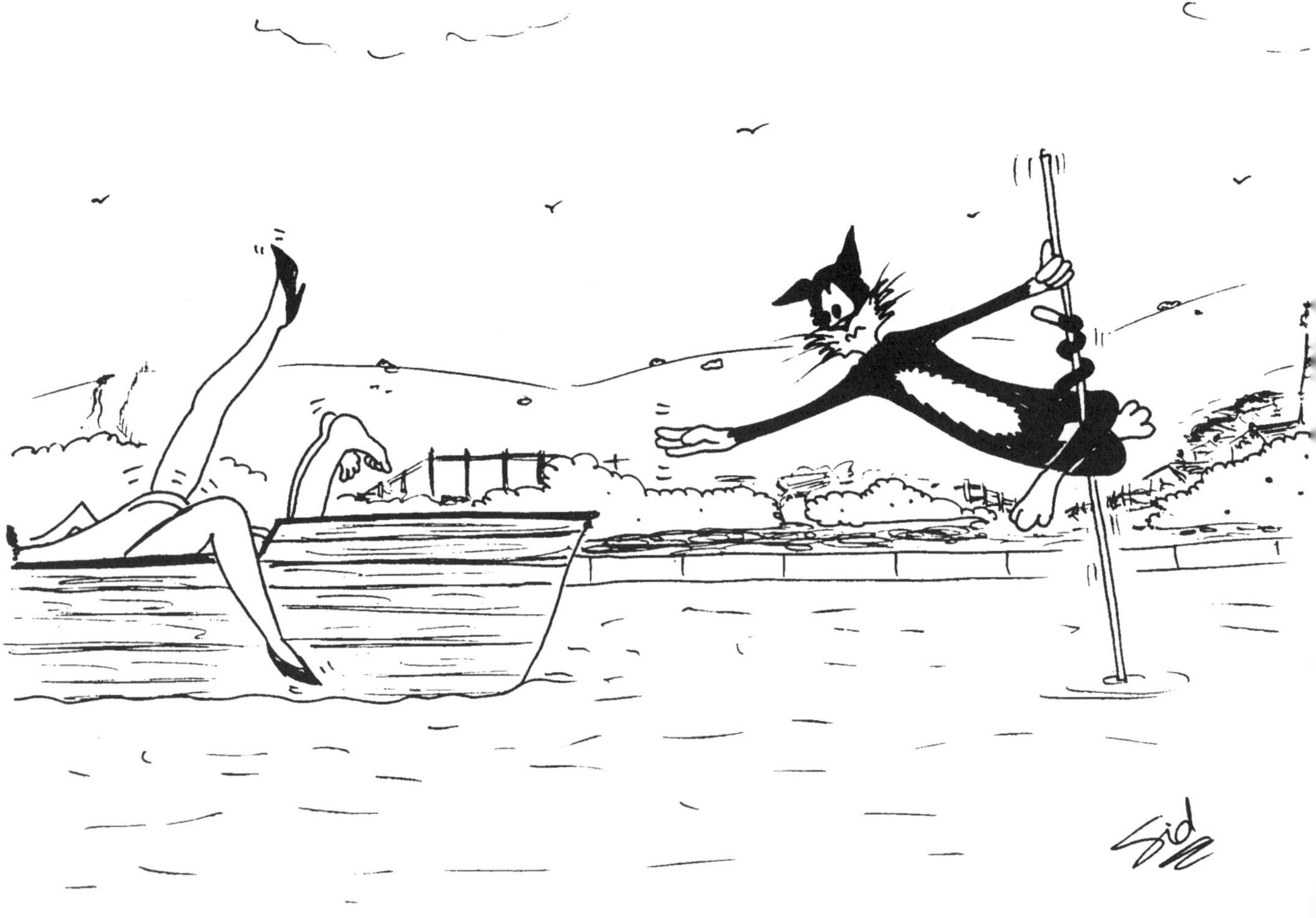
Sid

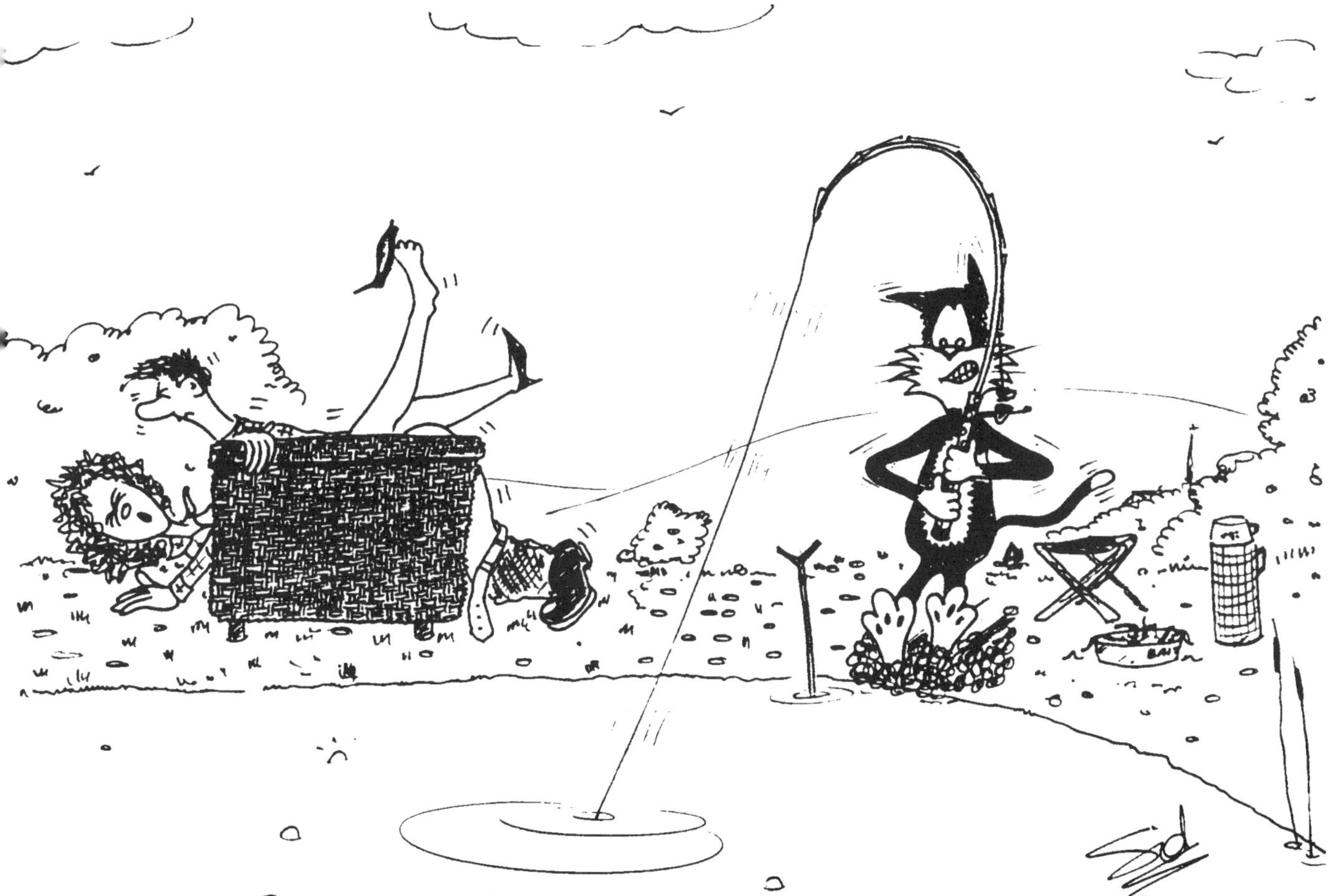

SILENCE.

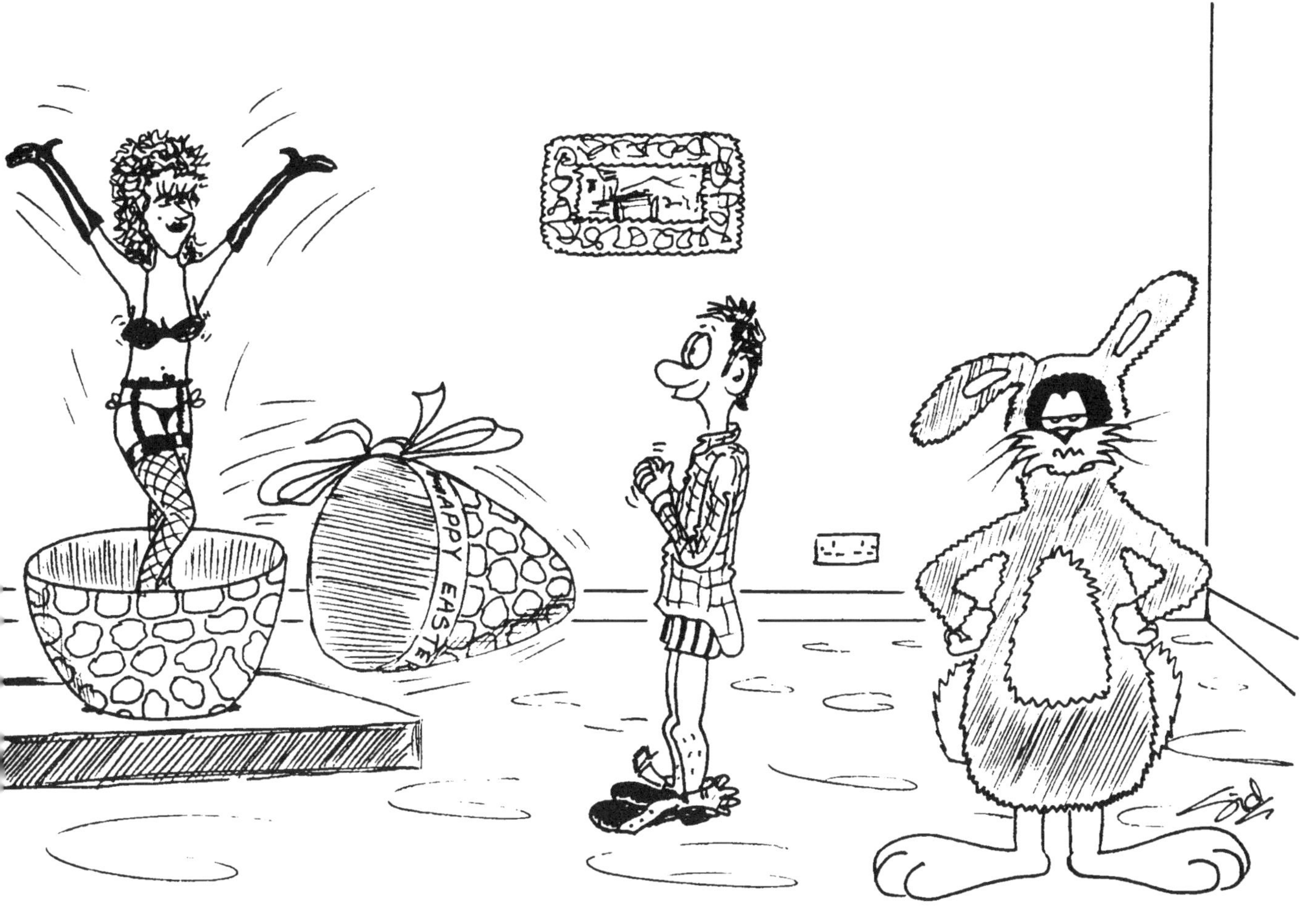
HAPPY EASTE

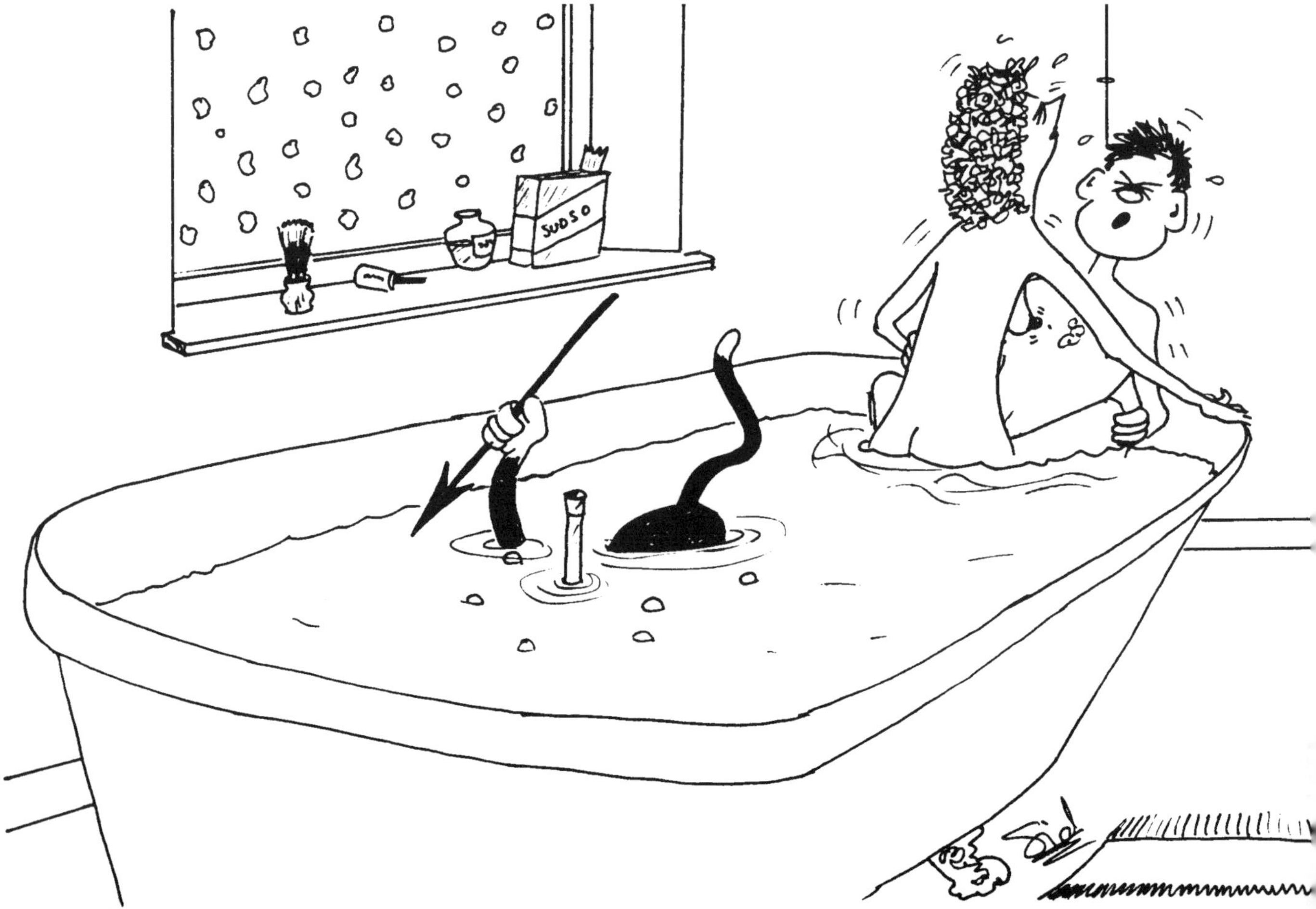
SUDSO

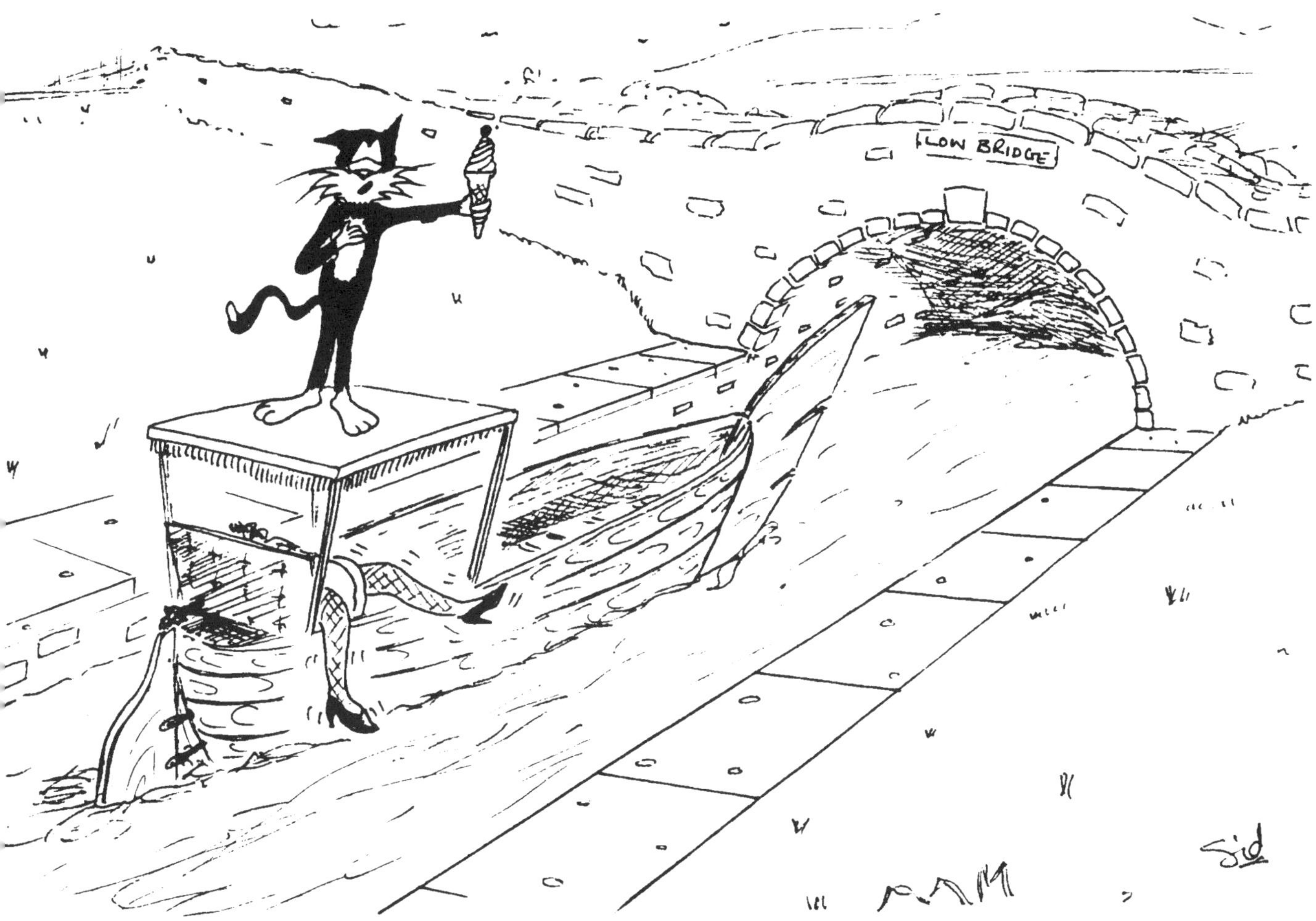
LOW BRIDGE
Sid

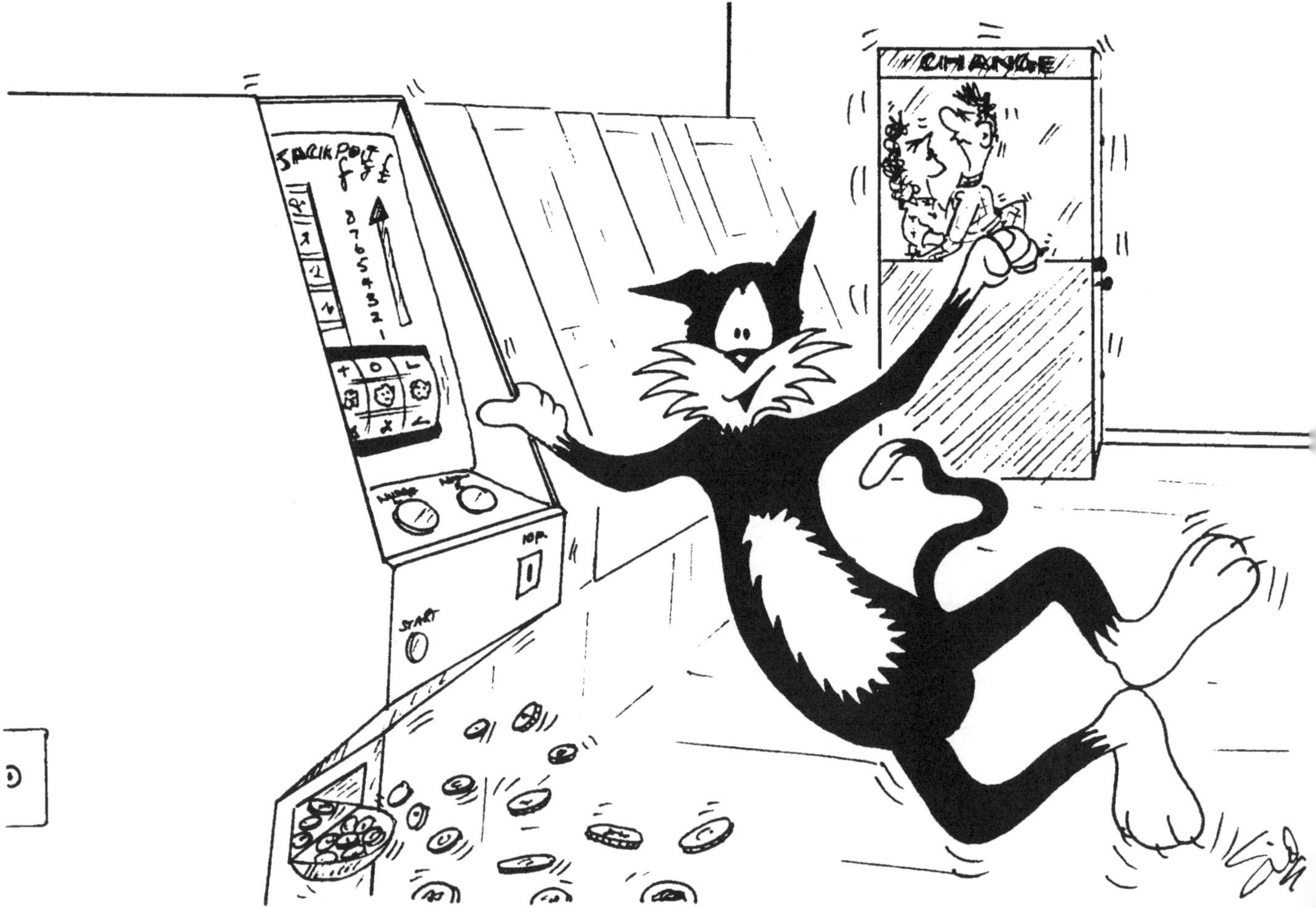
CHANGE
JACKPOT
START
10P.

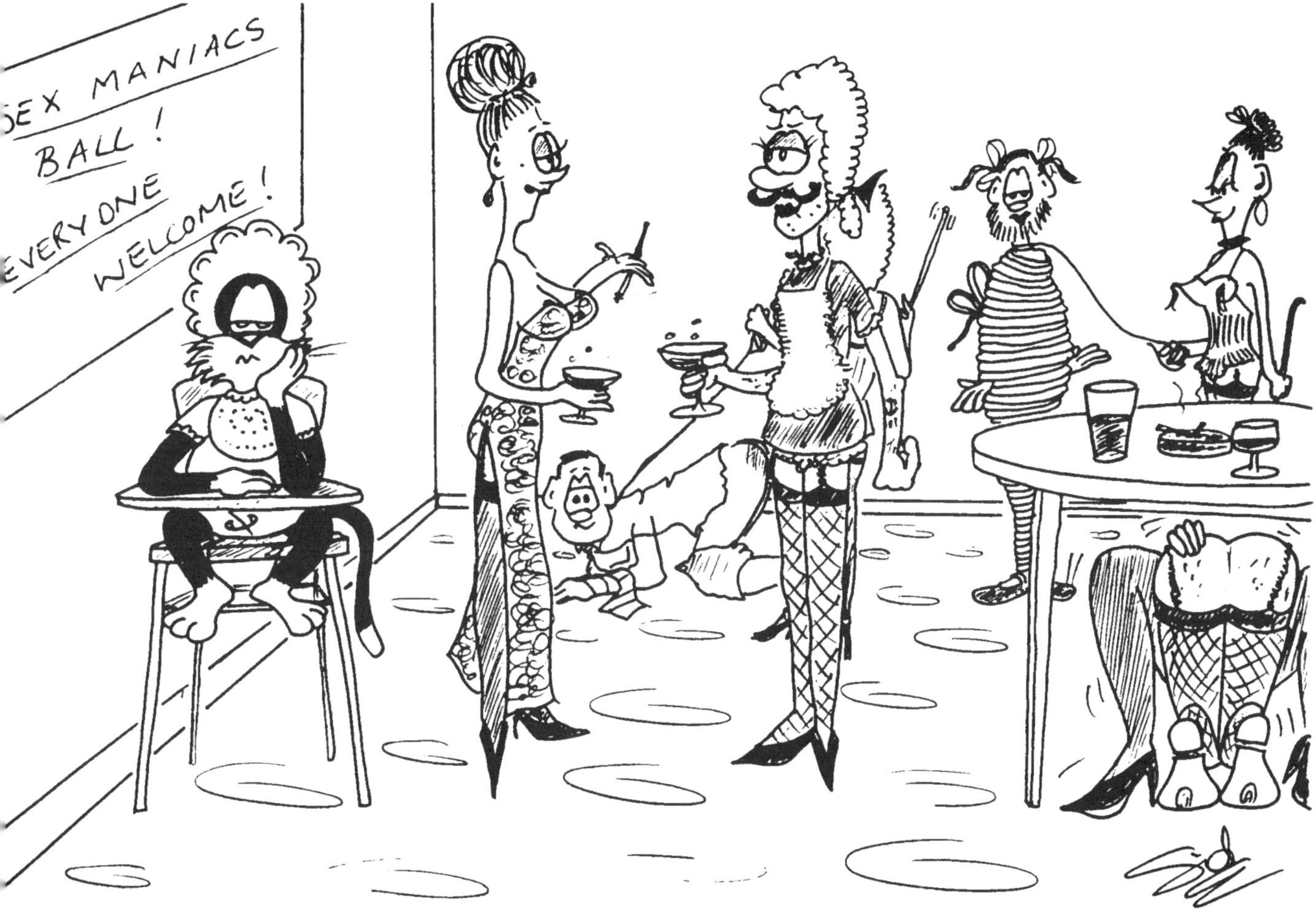
SEX MANIACS
BALL!
EVERYONE
WELCOME!

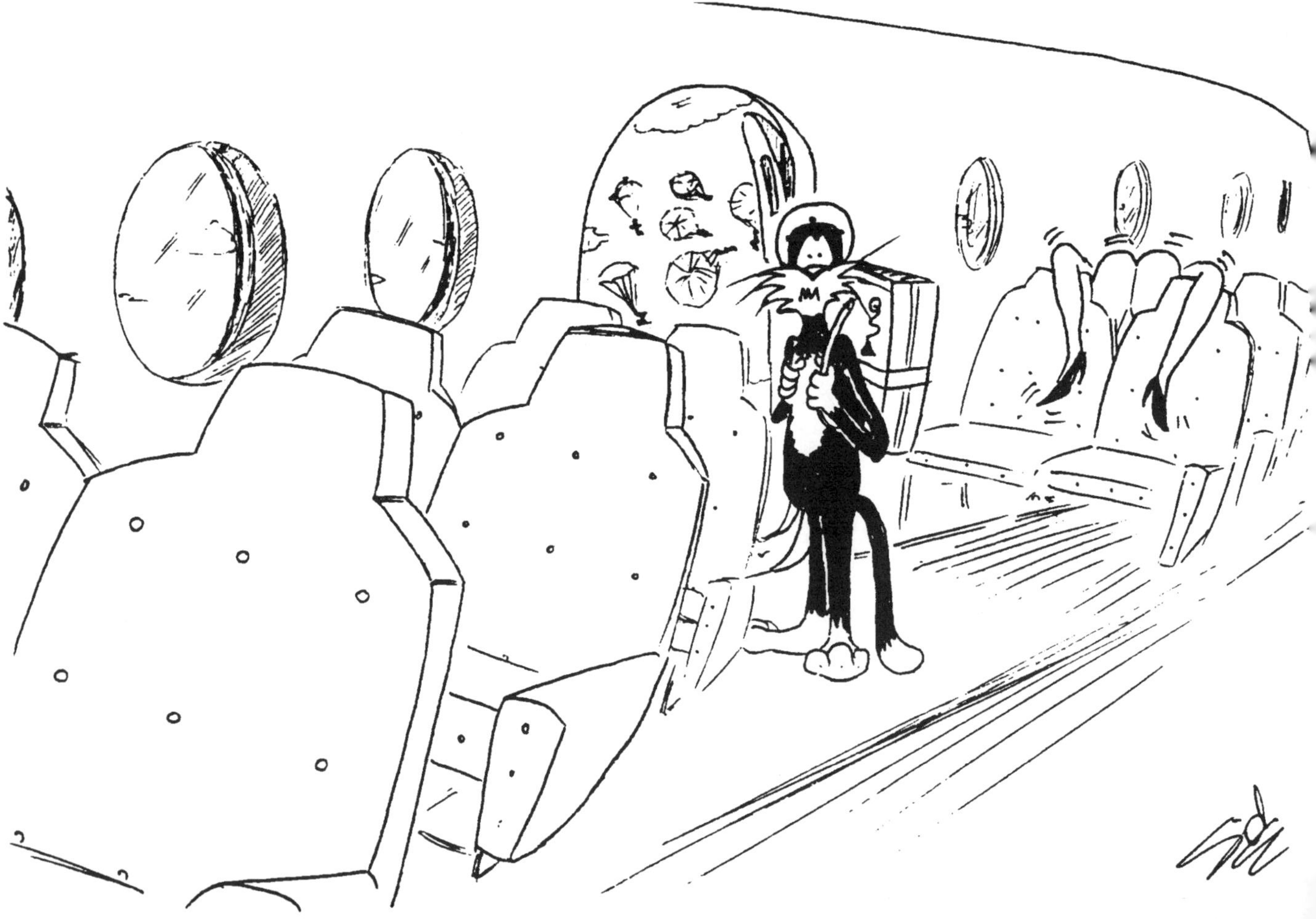

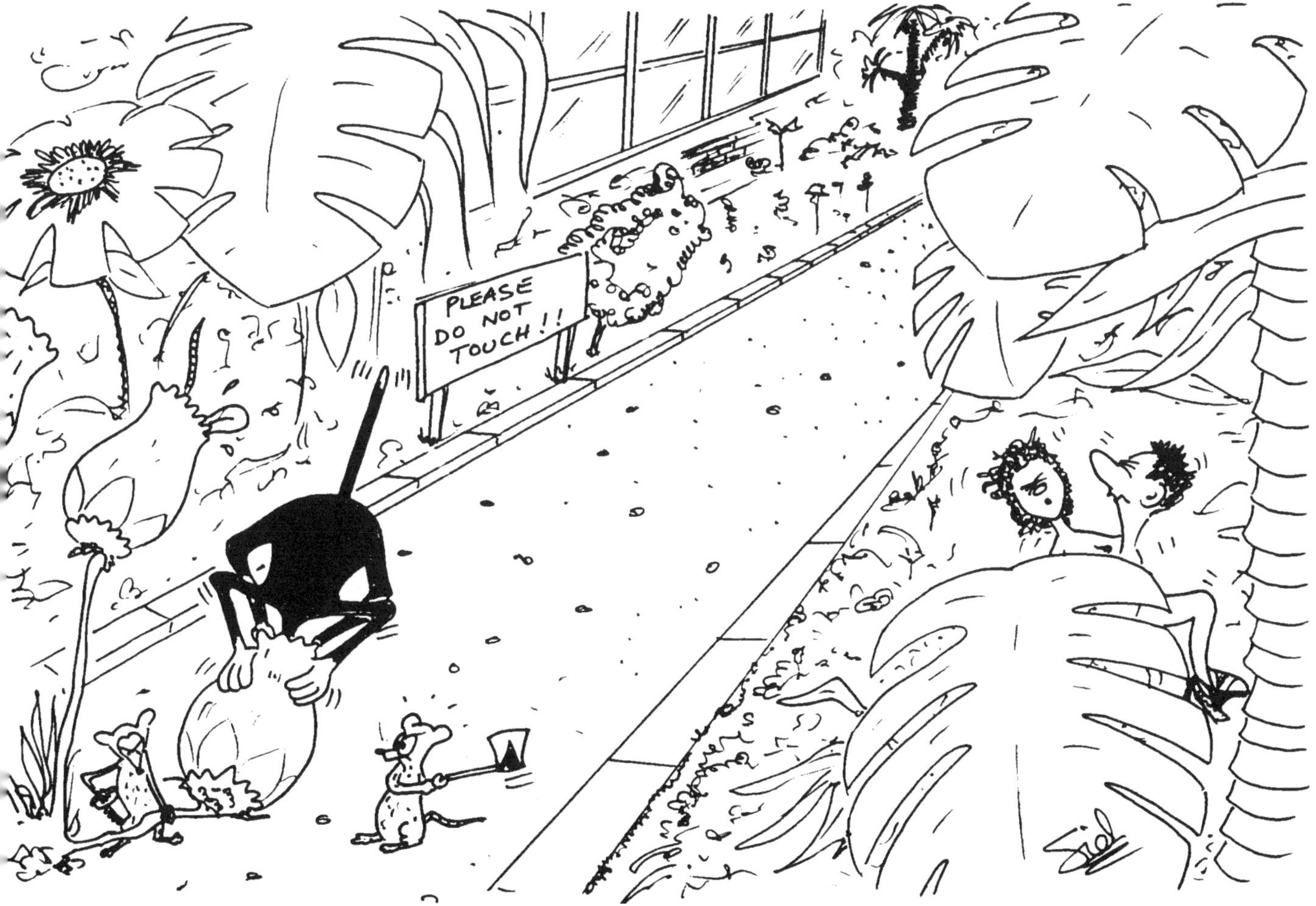
PLEASE
DO NOT
TOUCH!!

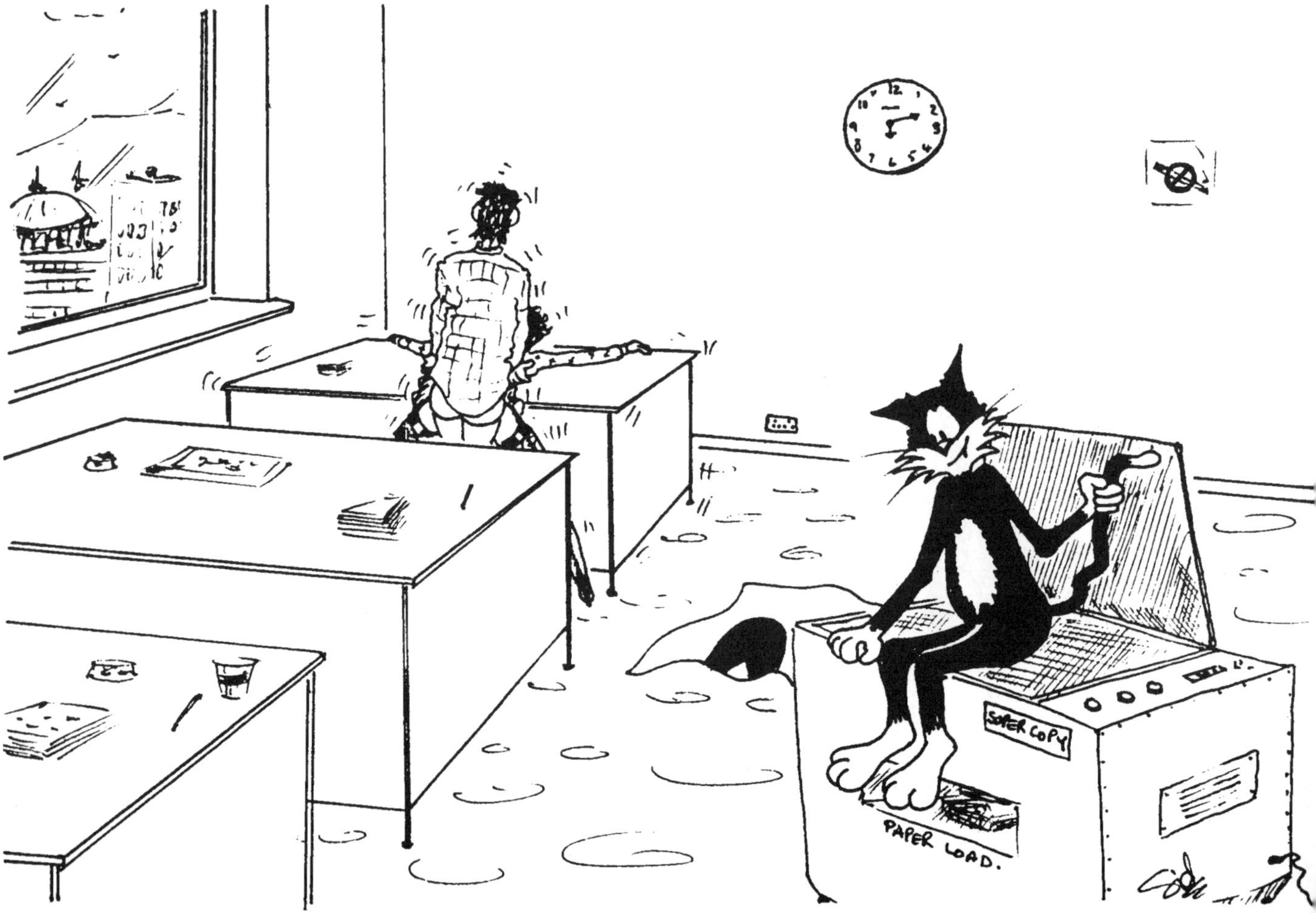
SUPER COPY
PAPER LOAD.

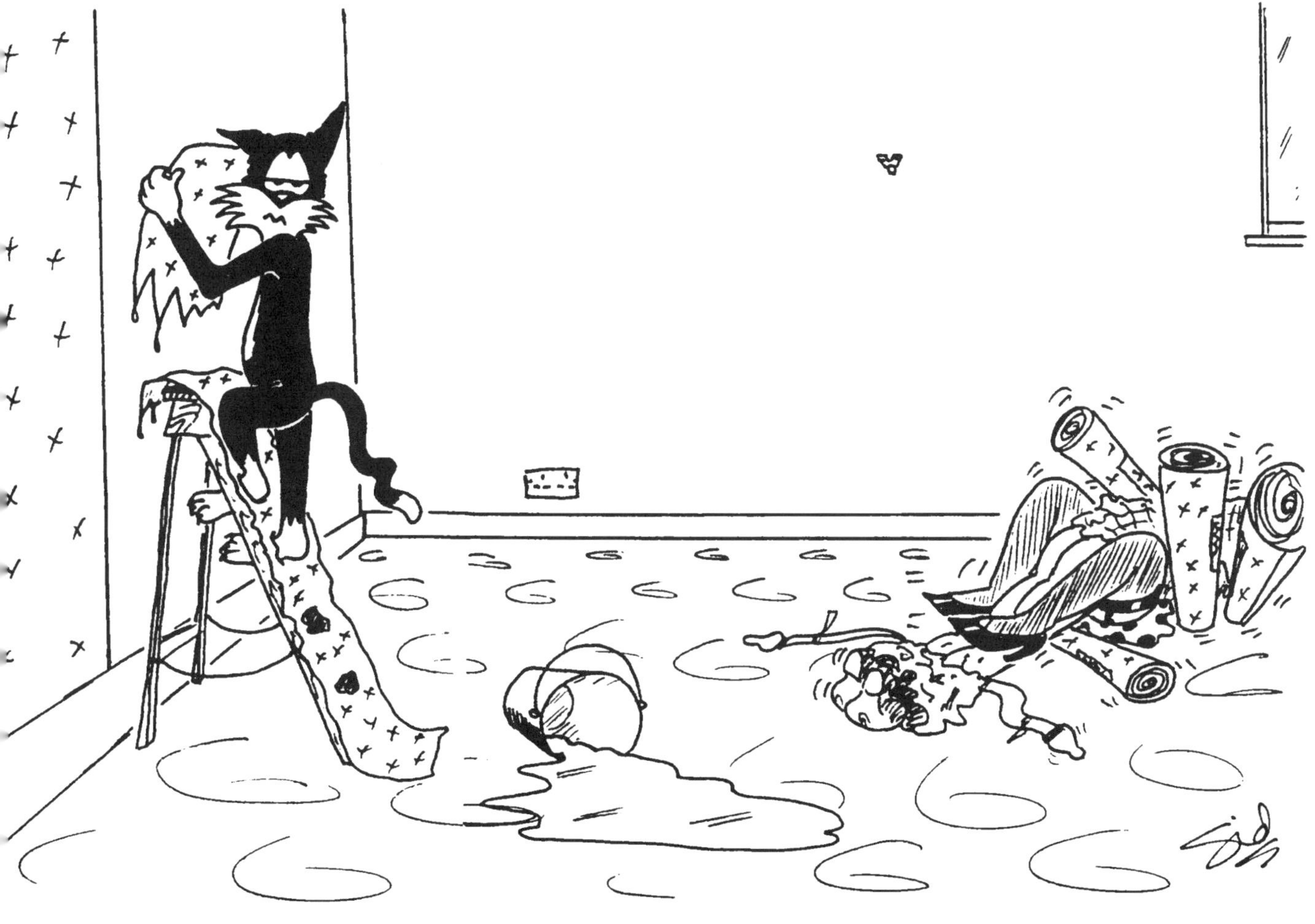
Sid

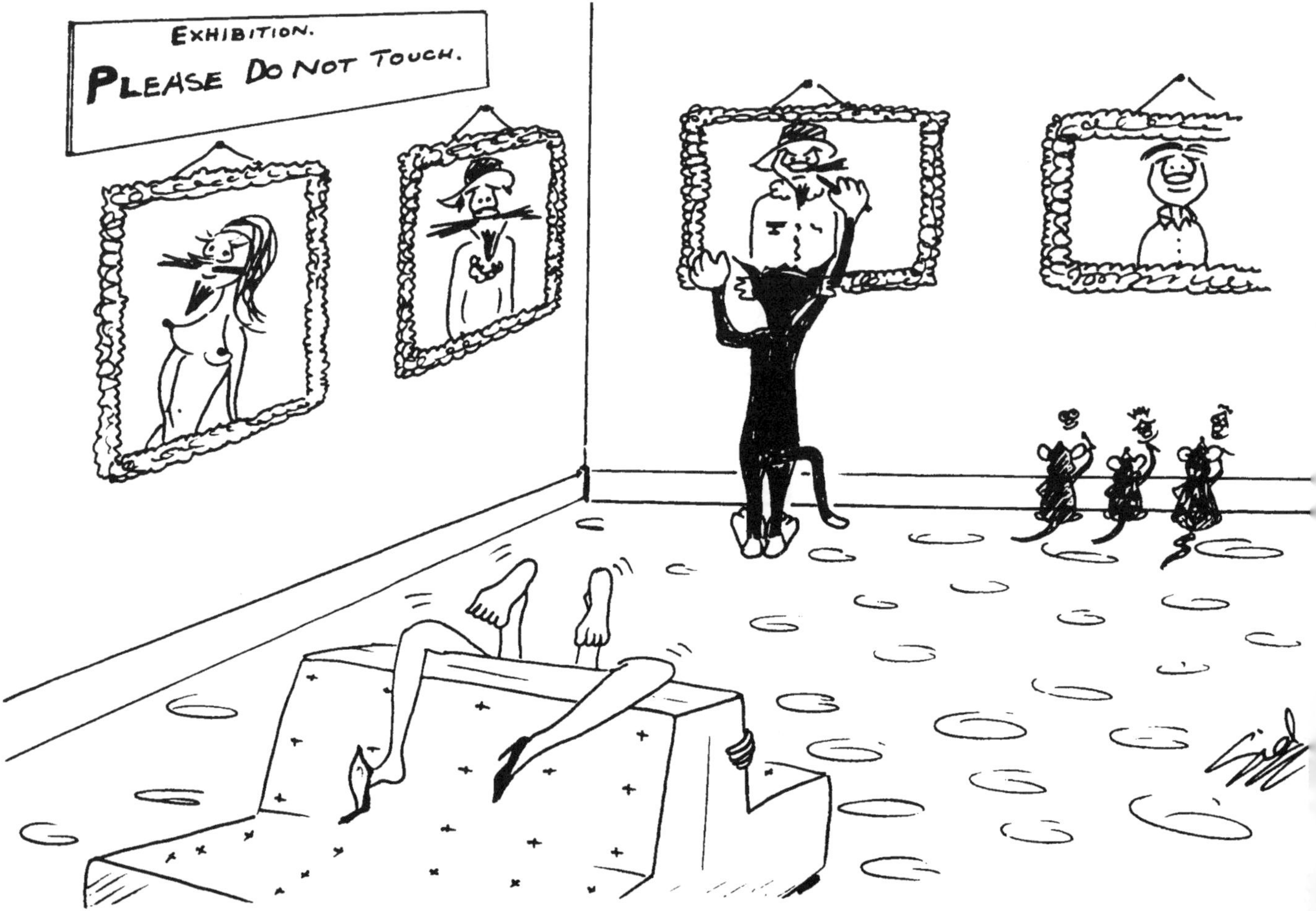
EXHIBITION.
PLEASE DO NOT TOUCH.

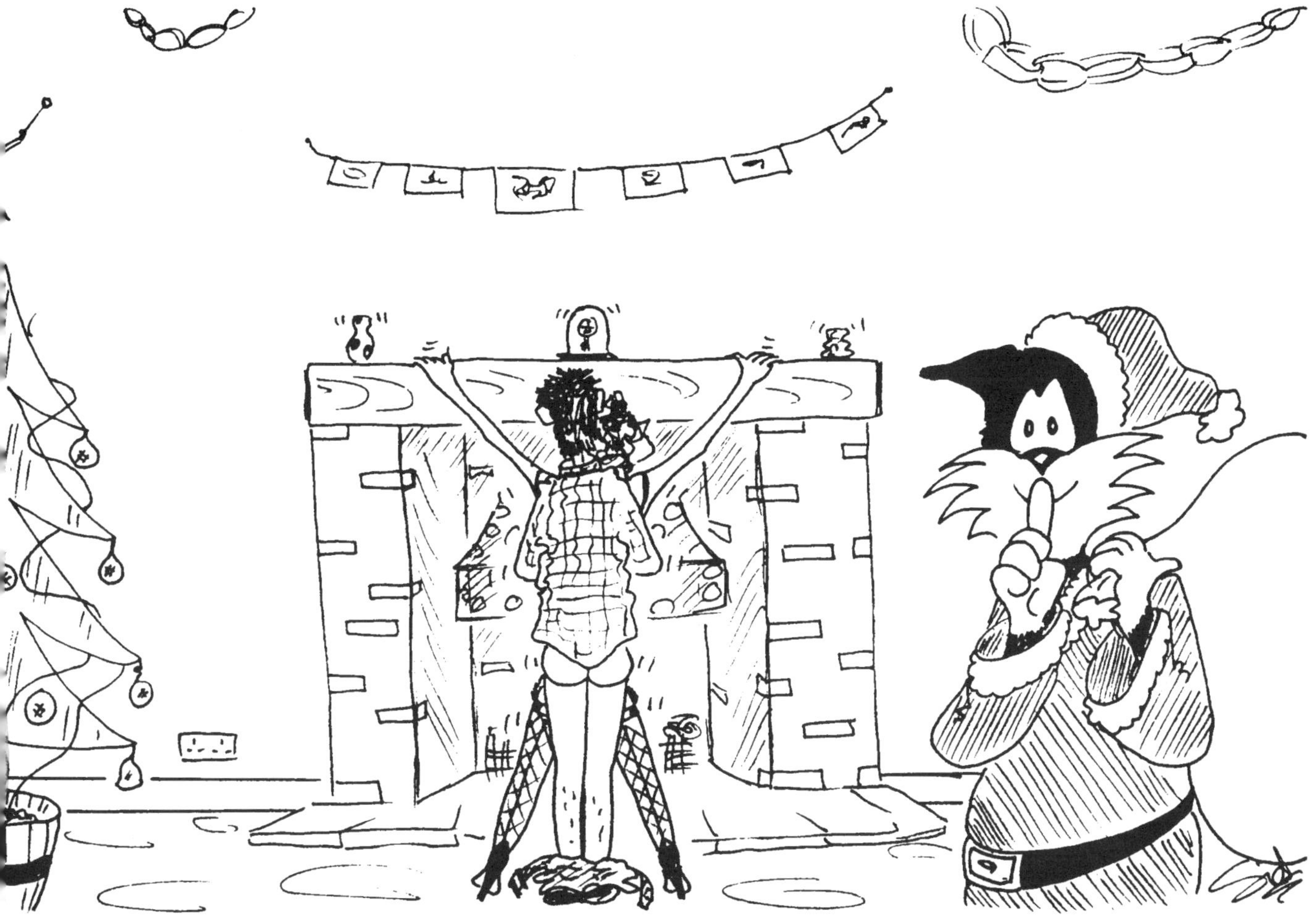

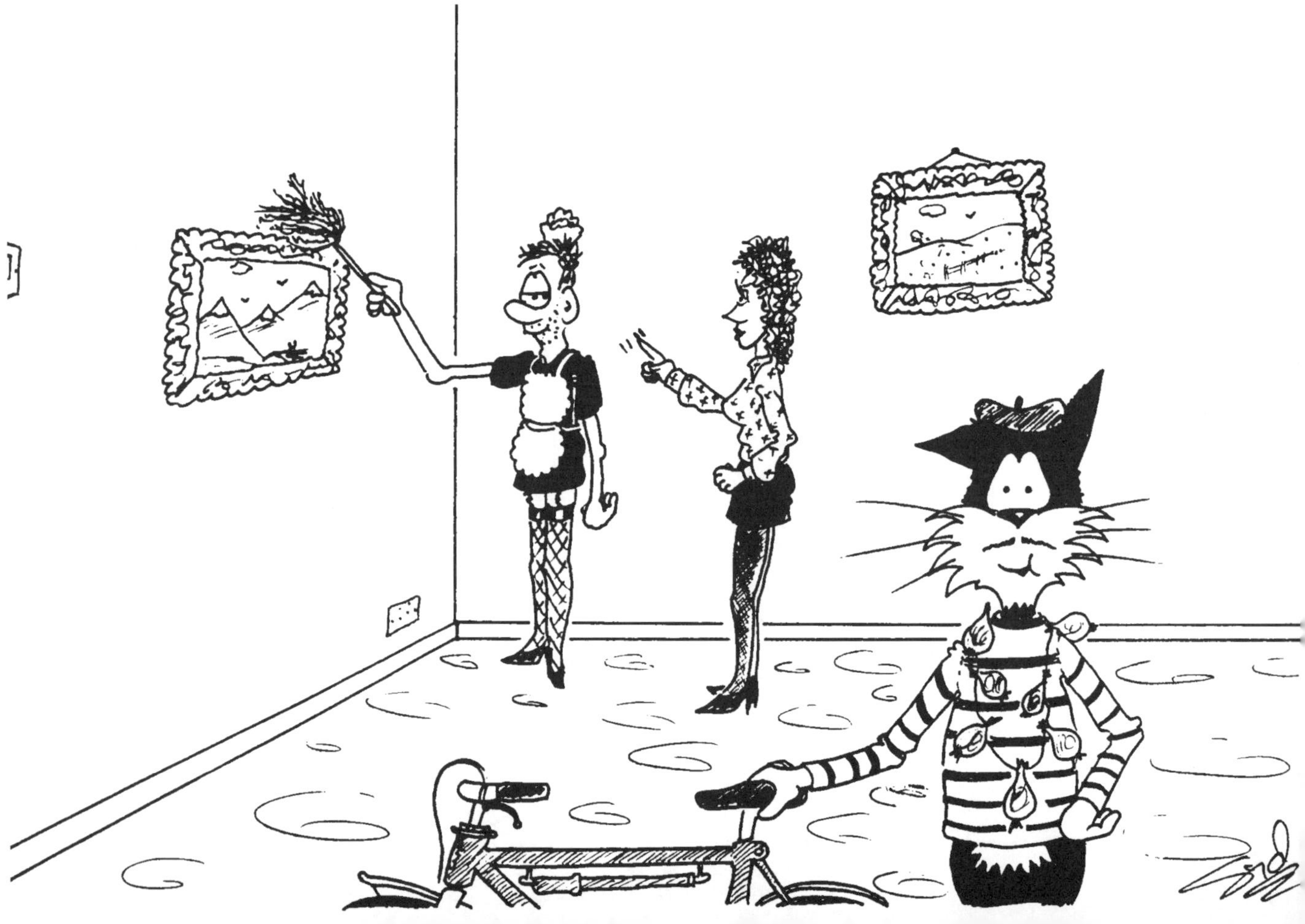

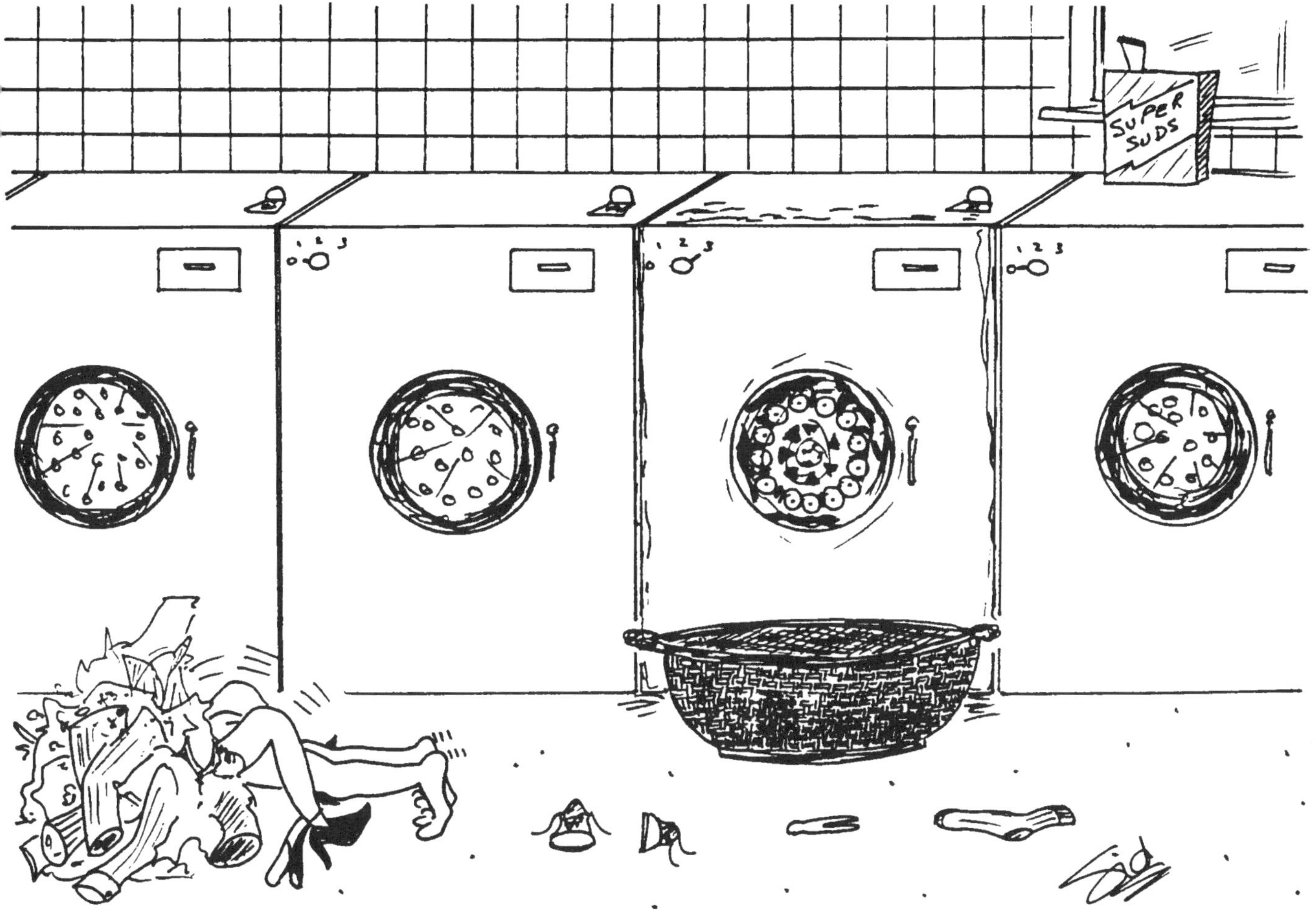
SUPER SUDS
1 2 3
1 2 3
1 2 3
Sid

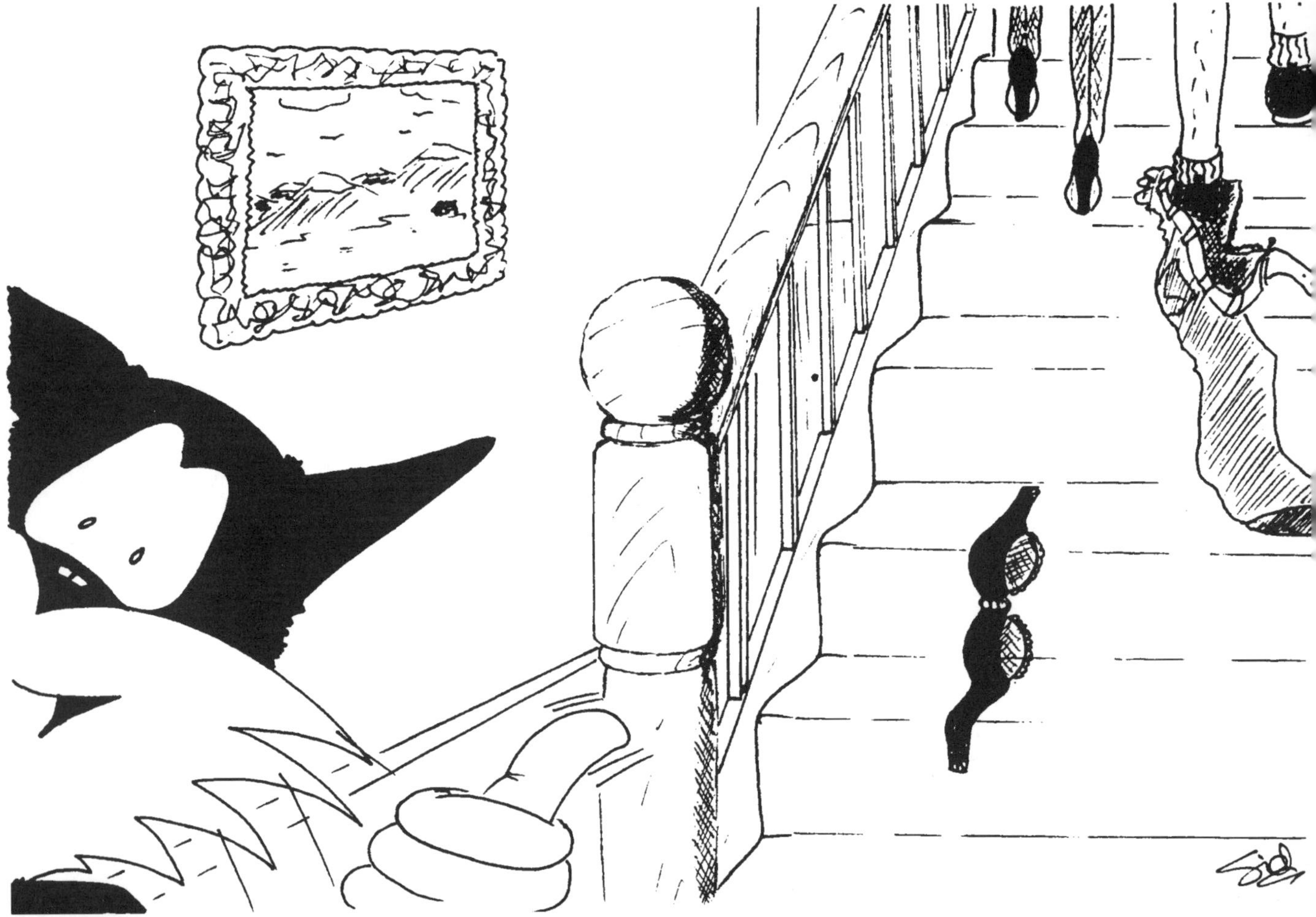

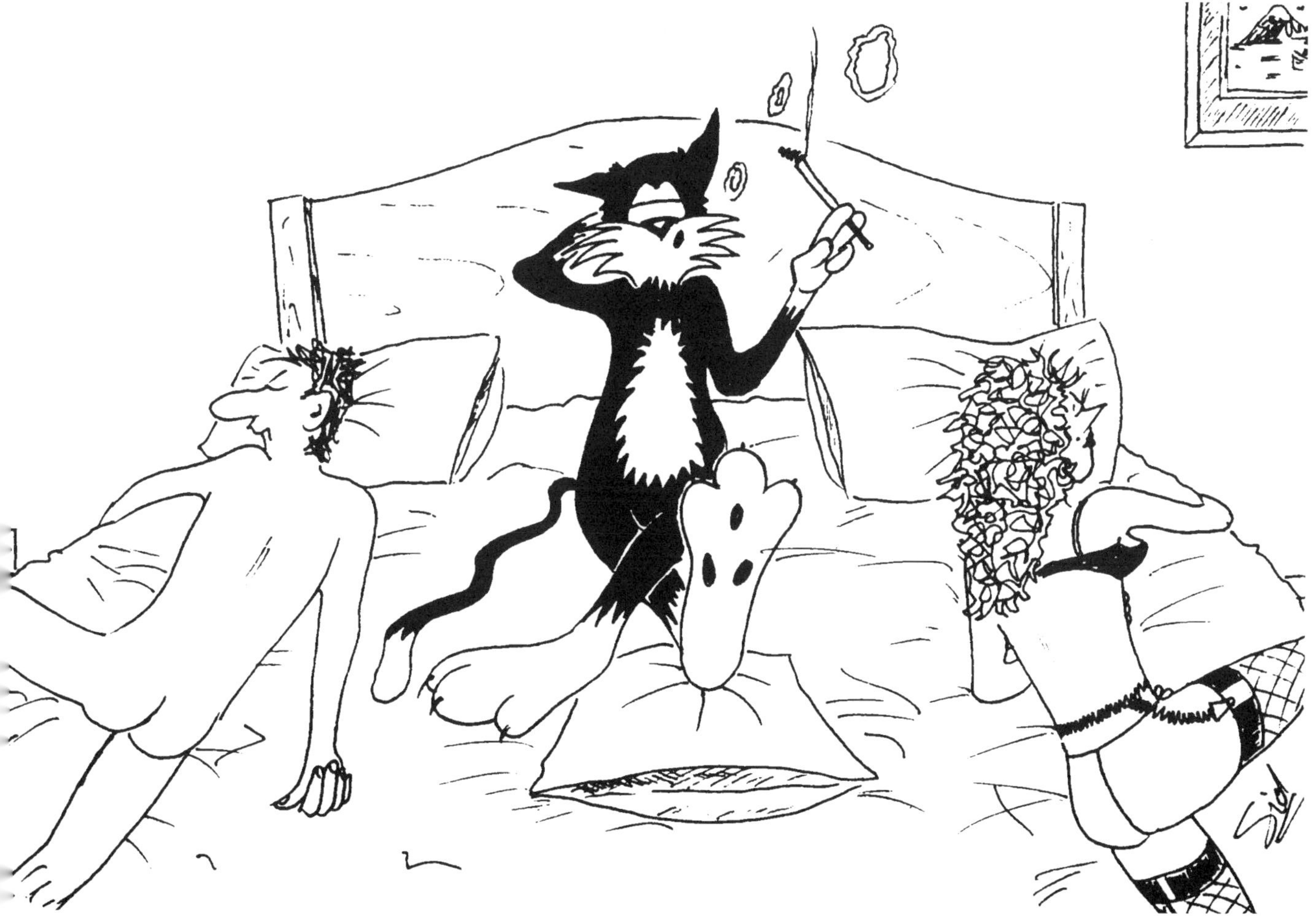

TITLES BY POWERFRESH
· NORTHAMPTON · ENGLAND ·

Please Send Me:

CRINKLED 'N' WRINKLED	£2.99	[ ]
DRIVEN CRAZY	£2.99	[ ]
OH NO ITS XMAS AGAIN	£2.99	[ ]
TRUE LOVE	£2.99	[ ]
IT'S A BOY	£2.99	[ ]
IT'S A GIRL	£2.99	[ ]
NOW WE ARE 40	£2.99	[ ]
FUNNY SIDE OF 30s	£2.99	[ ]
FUNNY SIDE OF 40 HIM	£2.99	[ ]
FUNNY SIDE OF 40 HER	£2.99	[ ]
FUNNY SIDE OF 50 HIM	£2.99	[ ]
FUNNY SIDE OF 50 HER	£2.99	[ ]
FUNNY SIDE OF 60'S	£2.99	[ ]
FUNNY SIDE OF SEX	£2.99	[ ]
THE COMPLETE BASTARDS GUIDE TO GOLF	£2.99	[ ]
SEX IS...	£2.99	[ ]
FOOTNOTES	£2.99	[ ]
SPLAT	£2.99	[ ]
WE'RE GETTING MARRIED	£2.99	[ ]
THE ART OF SLOBOLOGY	£2.99	[ ]
THE DEFINITIVE GUIDE TO VASECTOMY	£2.99	[ ]
KEEP FIT WITH YOUR CAT	£2.99	[ ]
MARITAL BLISS AND OTHER OXYMORONS	£2.99	[ ]
THE OFFICE FROM HELL	£2.99	[ ]
PMT CRAZED	£2.99	[ ]
SEXY CROTCHWORD PUZZLES	£2.99	[ ]
STONED AGE MAN	£2.99	[ ]
OUT TO LUNCH	£2.99	[ ]
HORNY MAN'S ADULT DOODLE BOOK	£2.50	[ ]
HORNY GIRL'S ADULT DOODLE BOOK	£2.50	[ ]
IF BABIES COULD TALK	£2.99	[ ]
CAT CRAZY	£2.99	[ ]
MAD TO TRAVEL BY AIR...	£2.99	[ ]
MAD TO PLAY GOLF...	£2.99	[ ]
MAD TO HAVE A BABY...	£2.99	[ ]
MAD TO GET MARRIED...	£2.99	[ ]
BUT IT HELPS		

I have enclosed cheque / postal order for £ .... made payable to **GUNNERS**

NAME..ADDRESS..

COUNTY..POSTCODE..

Please return to: Powerfresh Ltd. 3 Gray Street, Northampton, NN1 3QQ, ENGLAND.
EEC countries add £1 Postage, Packaging & Order processing. Outside EEC please add £3.00